In the December of 1626 a baby girl
was born to Queen Maria and King
Gustavus Adolphus of Sweden. The
King, who had desperately wanted a
son, declared that the child be educated
as a boy, and should eventually lead
Sweden into victory. So it was that
when her father died the little Princess
Christina was proclaimed 'King' at the
tender age of six-years-old.

Cursed with the outward trappings of a
male and the inward, violent emotions
of a female Christina stood alone
against the harsh criticism which her
strange appearance invited. Her decision
to abdicate caused a world sensation,
yet this was only a curtain-raiser to the
life of intrigue and gallantry which was
to follow – a life of many amorous
adventures and scandals which made
her THE OUTRAGEOUS QUEEN . . .

Also by Barbara Cartland

Books of Love, Life and Health
THE YOUTH SECRET
THE MAGIC OF HONEY
THE FASCINATING FORTIES
LOVE, LIFE AND SEX
MEN ARE WONDERFUL

Historical Biographies
THE SCANDALOUS LIFE OF KING CAROL
THE PRIVATE LIFE OF CHARLES II

and published by Corgi Books

Barbara Cartland

A Biography of Christina of Sweden

The Outrageous Queen

CORGI BOOKS
A DIVISION OF TRANSWORLD PUBLISHERS LTD

THE OUTRAGEOUS QUEEN

A CORGI BOOK o 552 09534 6

Originally published in Great Britain
by Frederick Muller Ltd.

PRINTING HISTORY

Frederick Muller edition published 1956
Frederick Muller second impression published 1956
Corgi edition published 1974

This book is set in 10 pt. Plantin

Corgi Books are published by
Transworld Publishers Ltd,
Cavendish House, 57–59 Uxbridge Road,
Ealing, London W.5.
Made and printed in Great Britain by
Cox & Wyman Ltd, London, Reading and Fakenham

The Outrageous Queen

FOREWORD

Any biographer is faced with a confusion of opinions about a controversial character, but none more diverse and contradictory than those which have been formed about Christina of Sweden, one of the most complex personalities of all time.

As will be found in this book, I have taken a very decided and often original line as regards her sexual activities and her personal reactions to people and events. But I have not invented anything and every situation is as true as research can make it.

The dialogue, too, is completely authentic, with the exception of a very few sentences which are introduced to lighten the story. These are, however, based on fact and are really historical reports translated into speech.

Readers who may be scandalized at Christina must remember that she lived in an age when everybody, and especially men, were unrestrained both morally and physically. With the pre-natal influence and the upbringing of a man and the sexual capabilities of a highly emotional woman, in an era of licence and excess, it is impossible to judge her by our standards and our conventions.

It would, however, be a hard heart which does not find something infinitely pathetic in this story of a lonely woman's desperate and courageous search for the truth.

July, 1955   BARBARA CARTLAND

CHAPTER ONE

THE man at the prow of the small coasting vessel wiped the salt spray from his myopic light blue eyes. He looked younger than his thirty-two years because of his remarkable fairness.

The pointed beard and close-cropped hair were light golden, the skin of his face and hands tanned by the open air, but as he stretched his arm to grip the side of the ship his forearm was as milky white and finely textured as a young girl's.

His great height was minimized by his immense breadth of shoulders and stocky frame.

In every movement there was strength – no one could wield an axe so strongly as he. Nor was his virility merely a matter of sudden quixotic outbursts of energy.

At times, when needs demanded, he had ridden one horse after another for fifteen hours at a stretch.

He was clad in a badly stained buff coat and dark pantaloons, with boots of soft Russian leather. On the back of his head was a dirty beaver hat.

A hundred thousand soldiers of his country wore exactly the same clothes. But there was one difference. Around his waist was tied a crumpled and slightly torn scarlet sash – the emblem of royalty.

The man in the boat was Gustavus Adolphus, King of Sweden.

'*Il re d'oro*' of his Italian mercenaries, 'Lion of the North' to his Swedish subjects, 'Gideon and Elias' to the Protestants of Europe, 'the Lion from Midnight' to his Catholic enemies from the sunny south.

'The Servant of God' to himself – and one of the greatest heroes of Europe to his contemporaries and to history.

On this November afternoon in 1626 he was returning from a tour of the defences which were dotted along the coast and on the islands which stretched eastwards from the Royal City of Stockholm.

He ignored the bitter wind which was sweeping straight from Russia, heralding the cold to come. As always when he approached his beloved capital he pondered on the past and dreamed of the future.

Seen from the sea the city seemed to be a floating fortress, with the waters of the Baltic and the ice-blue Lake Malar marrying at the base of the rocks on which it was built.

Nearly four hundred years before a great Swedish king, Birger Jarl, had in his wisdom chosen this spot as capable of nourishing a city so impregnable that neither pirates nor land-borne enemies could overrun it.

Even more strongly impressed in the King's mind was the day when his ancestor, another Gustavus, founder of the Vasa dynasty, had a century before made a state entry into the capital.

It was on Midsummer Eve in 1523 that he brought his people news of victory over the Danes.

At that time, even though every man, woman and child were out in the streets to meet him, there were only three thousand to show their gratitude and pride.

Since then the city had grown vigorously. Foreign traders and craftsmen had settled there.

The peasants and aristocrats alike had moved from the country to breathe life into the sombre fabric of fortress, mansion and croft.

As the vessel rounded a small headland the King saw the bustle of activity on the western side of the town.

A year earlier the whole area had been gutted by fire. Now, by His Majesty's edict, foreign craftsmen from the great building nations of Europe were creating a modern city.

There were wide streets crossing at right angles, magnificent houses in the process of being erected, and a new Royal Palace.

The vessel passed the Kransen, the cordon with its booms that protected the quays of the island. Ahead the palace rose straight out of the water on the north-east corner. Massive walls, eighteen feet thick, stretched out like long arms and guarded the keep called the Three Crowns.

The King's journey was over. The vessel bumped against the quay and he jumped ashore.

A crowd of soldiers and citizens had come through the Saint Nikali Gate to welcome him. Without ceremony he greeted them as familiar friends and hurried on foot along the narrow, twisting streets, through the Great Market and to the great doors of the palace.

A wide archway led to the untidy courtyard surrounded by the massive walls of the Royal apartments, the stabling and the Councillors' rooms towering up four and five storeys on every side.

As soon as the King had impatiently pushed away the lackeys who crowded round him, he saw the person he most desired to meet.

An aged man clad in the long black cloak of an astrologer stood a little aloof from the others, as if the very mystery of his rites segregated him from the commonplace.

No one in the palace, not even the Chancellor Axel Oxenstierna himself, was permitted such intimate contact with the King as this seer.

'News?' the King demanded brusquely.

'We are entering the period of Sagittarius, Your Majesty, and the signs show that there will be a Prince of Vasa before Capricorn.'

The King nodded.

'I believe that. I have had a strange dream. I saw St. George fight the dragon. The image was like the wooden carving of the battle which you have seen in the Storkyrkan. But the face of St. George was a face in the image of my Queen. This time she will bear a son.'

The Astrologer raised a warning hand.

'Yes, Sire,' he said, moving closer to the King, 'but there are ominous signs as well. The birth has death as its companion. Perhaps to Her Majesty our Queen Maria Eleanora; perhaps, Sire – to you.'

'Might it be the child?'

There was the sudden chill of apprehension and fear in the King's voice.

'It could be, Sire,' the Astrologer replied. 'Yet if it lives a day and a night then it will be great and famous.'

'He – not it,' the King corrected. 'You will recall that the child was conceived in war. It was when the Queen came to greet me at Reval that this blessing came to us. I was weary from the Polish wars and little did I think as we crossed to Finland that at last there would be an heir to the throne of my country.'

All that summer Gustavus Adolphus had been a sick man.

He had suffered from malaria, and he had cursed his body in that it had failed to serve his desire to extend the little kingdom of Sweden into one of the great empires of Europe.

His illness had forced him to remain in his own country during the warm months as he was attacked by fever after fever.

Intensely superstitious, he had wondered if his own weakness would have been communicated to the child, so that once again Queen Maria Eleanora would bear a weakling as she had done on two previous occasions.

The girl children to which she had given birth had lived for only a few days. But this time the astrologers of the Court confirmed his dreams and his ambitions.

On December 7th, 1626, as snow floated down over the city of Stockholm, the Queen took to her bed.

For hour after hour the King stood staring out of the window where below in the courtyard hundreds of his people waited in the cold for news.

He made no attempt to see his wife, for he was, in fact, afraid of her.

The marriage had been a fiery romance which had soon burned itself out. Gustavus Adolphus had swept into Brandenburg and virtually abducted the Lutheran princess, the elopement being connived at by her mother and in face of the violent opposition of her brother, the King of Poland.

The tall and slender girl had been a timid but acquiescent bride. But soon she defaced and spoiled the King's love by a domineering attitude and petulant outbursts of temperament.

She was a woman who had no qualities beyond her sexual charms, and she was jealous of any other interest that occupied her husband.

She hated his adoration for his country, and despised his subjects' affection for him.

Seeking to dictate by love, she therefore destroyed its efficacy. And when she found that her passion could not force into being the last invincible weapon – the gift of a son to her husband – she became shrewish and neurotic.

So fantastic was her behaviour that it was as if she tried to destroy the last vestiges of all that had once meant everything in her life.

After six years of marriage she still retained much of her youthful beauty. Her face was a perfect oval, her features delicately chiselled, her skin clear and unblemished, but her eyes, which had once been dark with desire, now had always the wildness of hysteria in them.

They moved continually in restless fright, and her upbringing had aggravated her emotional instability.

As is so often the case with children whose tempers are uncertain, she had been pandered to, and spoilt. More than that, she had never really loved her husband, although her desire had been a passionate lustful fire.

Now her feeling for him was really one of dislike, and she disliked her adopted country even more.

One of her first remarks made in a loud and hysterical voice at the finest banquet that the Palace of Stockholm had ever known, had fomented the hatred of the Swedish courtiers from the first weeks of her marriage.

'I would rather have bread and water anywhere in the world,' she said petulantly, 'than Royal food in Sweden.'

Early in their married life the King, who could always find a method of achieving conquest over his enemies in war and politics, discovered that he was helpless to deal with a woman who burst into tears whenever she was thwarted.

When she had miscarriages and gave birth to children who died almost immediately, the mutual apathy increased. The marriage became a travesty of everything that this deeply affectionate man had envisaged.

But now it seemed that she was at last going to present him with a son.

He felt, for the first time in years, an affection and a tenderness for his wife. But his old dread of her temper prevented him from entering the bedchamber and making any gesture of sympathy.

Then, just as the short day died he heard, loud and strident, the cry of a baby.

It was a cry which seemed to have a guttural, deep tone to it and the King smiled with delight. Only a male child could make such a cry. Still he did not enter the room.

A door opened and a lady-in-waiting came hurrying to his side.

'A son has been born to you, Your Majesty,' she said.

The King nodded and walked quickly to the hall. There the Burgomaster of the town and priests were awaiting his orders. They were simple.

'Let the bells be rung,' he commanded triumphantly.

Within minutes the bells were clanging the news of a Royal heir across the town, and the message was taken up in the hamlets and villages on either side of the water.

But they were proclaiming a lie. The child was a girl.

When the midwives delivered the baby, it was covered with a caul from head to foot. It cried before the caul had been removed, and it was this cry that had convinced them all, even as it convinced the King, that the baby was a Prince.

The new Princess was an unprepossessing infant covered all over with a dark down. She was dark, almost swarthy in appearance, strong and angular in physique. The consternation in the bedchamber when the sex of the newly born child was realized was profound.

None of the palace staff dared to tell the King that a mistake had been made.

But the King's sister, Catharine, who was more intimate with Gustavus than any living person, agreed to break the news.

She wrapped the baby in a single blanket, and, taking it in her arms, walked to the hall where the King, oblivious of the bitter wind, was standing at the open door listening to the bells.

'Here is your child,' she said, abruptly handing him the baby.

He looked down at the little naked body, and without a tremor of emotion, took the child gently in his arms.

'Let us thank God, sister,' he said. 'I hope this girl child will be as good as a boy to me. May God preserve her now that He has sent her.'

'You are disappointed; that we all know,' the Princess whispered, 'but you must remember that you are still young, and Eleanora has many years in which to bear you an heir. You must not believe that this child will inherit the throne of Sweden.'

The King shook his head.

'My sister, I am quite satisfied,' he told her. 'May God preserve her to me.'

He handed back the baby and walked slowly to his own apartments, calling to the ever-attendant Astrologer to follow him.

Catharine returned to the bedchamber and told the worried midwives that, strangely and unexpectedly, Gustavus had shown no anger. The mother, lying tearfully and embittered on her bed, refused at first to nurse the child.

'I am cursed in this country,' she said. 'My every wish is refused, and now the whole Palace and the town is filled with false joy – a joy I do not feel myself. I prayed for a son and instead I get an ugly daughter.'

In the King's apartments, the Astrologer shuffled uneasily, conscious, like all those of his craft, that he had reached the dangerous point where his prophecies had been revealed as untrue. But the King seemed unbelievably cheerful.

'Go you and decide whether the death you forecast is mine,' he ordered. 'It may be so but I feel remarkably well. As for the baby – I cannot believe that such a vigorous child can die before a day and a night have gone. As for the Queen . . .'

He broke off as if her life or death was now of little account. For a moment he was silent, contemplating once again the change that had come into his life now that he had a Royal daughter. Quite suddenly he laughed aloud.

'She will undoubtedly be a clever woman,' he said, 'for even at her birth she has succeeded in deceiving us all.'

Apart from the fact that Sweden – forever engaged in wars – would have been better served by a warrior king, there was no constitutional crisis because the heir to the throne was a girl.

More than twenty years earlier during the reign of Karl IX both monarch and people had agreed that the eldest unmarried daughter of the Royal House could succeed to the throne if there was no male heir.

The day and the night passed. The Astrologers repeated their prophecies that the baby would indeed be great.

Only the Queen continued to hate the amazingly strong baby she had borne. She turned away almost with loathing every time the baby was brought to her, and after a day or two no further attempts were made to place her child in her arms.

With a pouting of her petulant mouth and a look of furious resentment in her eyes, she would recount the baby's faults to anyone who would listen.

'She is dark like an African: look at her enormous nose. And why should my child have black eyes when her father's and mine are blue? She is big and gawky and I do not like ugly things. I do not want to see her – take her away!'

The King neither knew nor cared about his wife's attitude. Before Christmas he had organized his daughter's baptism.

'She shall be called Christina after my mother,' he ordered. 'If she is wise and brave as she was, then Sweden will indeed be blessed.'

At the ceremony in the great old church of Stockholm it was said that a significant incident occurred.

Despite the ruthless action which had been taken against the Catholic religion many relics of it remained. Some who were near the officiating clergyman believed that he broke faith with the Lutheran religion by making the sign of the Cross on the baby's forehead, with fingers dipped in holy water that he had concealed near the altar.

If this was true the King did not see it, and indeed no one mentioned the fact until many years later when Christina's religious beliefs contributed to the tragedy and triumph of her life.

The baby continued to thrive. She was both remarkably strong and outstandingly intelligent. The gawkiness which had incensed her mother did not entirely disappear but was not very noticeable because of her grace.

Gustavus, for the first time in his life, neglected his State duties in order to watch his child for hours at a time.

The very day after her birth he had called an assembly of the Estates, in which the country was asked to recognize his daughter as heir to the throne, with all the members of the Council swearing allegiance to her.

He was anxious to have this matter settled because he knew that very soon the call of war would have to be answered and he would have to leave his heir in the care of servants. There was also the chance that he might meet death on the field of battle.

He had other worries.

Although the courtiers were afraid to approach him and speak outright on such a delicate subject, he knew that within the Palace itself Christina had formidable enemies.

There was still a handful of intimates from Brandenburg whose first loyalty was to the Queen and not to Sweden. With their help, Maria Eleanora began a campaign of hatred against the baby which was not only unnatural but indicative of her incipient madness.

The efforts she made to destroy her child were conceived with the cunning of a mentally unstable woman.

When Christina was only a few months old a heavy beam

16

fixed with all the efficiency of people skilled in the construction of wooden houses unaccountably fell from the ceiling and crashed on her cradle.

Fortunately the cradle itself was robustly constructed of oak and it took the main impact before the hood and sides were shattered, but the beam came to rest against her shoulder and the baby was seriously bruised.

Efforts were made to conceal the reasons for the accident from the King, and he remained ignorant of this direct attempt at murder.

Not long afterwards, there occurred what was perhaps a genuine accident, for the woman concerned was a Swede and not a German. Christina was dropped by her wet nurse on the stone flags of the floor.

Fortunately the child did not fall on her head, but her shoulder was dislocated and the flesh torn. For the rest of her life she was slightly disfigured with the blade of one shoulder sticking out so that her neck was held a little sideways.

It was one of those accidents which have a tremendous impact on a young life.

Years afterwards Christina said that even though she was a matter of months old at the time, she recalled vividly how her mother laughed when the nurse, panic-stricken, rushed in to confess that she had been so careless.

These were only two of a score of peculiar occurrences which might have destroyed Christina or turned her into a useless cripple.

Whether they were all deliberate or whether she was a particularly unlucky baby cannot now be known.

The fact remains that Christina in the first year of her life was protected by a most tenacious guardian Angel from an unprecedented number of risks.

CHAPTER TWO

THE year of Christina's birth was a milestone in the career of Gustavus Adolphus – and not solely because the succession to the throne was assured.

He could regard this period as a summit of his greatness, even though his ambitious eyes still looked with restless longing to the Baltic horizon and the lands beyond it whose riches and strategic importance tempted his warrior mind.

When he became King in 1611 his father, Karl IX, handed him a proud nation still angry at real or imagined wrongs.

The Council of the Kingdom, which represented all the great families of the country, had been the violent enemy of Karl, and as they were the most powerful and wealthy group in the country – with infinitely greater resources than the Royalist Party – for a time the issue was in doubt.

Karl IX made a ruthless attack on them in 1600, when, as a result of carefully arranged trials, a number of the most powerful nobles were executed.

But Karl was more than a ruthless man. He was a brilliant organizer and in his lifetime he raised the poverty-stricken kingdom to a position of some wealth and influence.

The rewards of his work would have been still greater if he had not been almost continually involved in wars with Russia, Denmark and Poland.

When Gustavus Adolphus came to the throne he continued the dictatorial policy of his father, but as he was a far more brilliant soldier, the menace of Sweden's enemies diminished rapidly.

In 1613 he regained Älvsborg, a vital port which gave the country a gateway to the North Sea. It was true that the price he had to pay to the Danes was a ransom which temporarily depleted Sweden's finances and caused bitter criticism from the already impoverished nobles, but it was a price well worth paying.

Next he turned against Russia, and in 1617 the first signs

of the greatness of his reign appeared, for large areas were ceded to Sweden, with the result that Russia was excluded from the Baltic for generations to come.

His military victories were all the more important because in Sweden proper the population was under a million, and the country's lack of wealth prevented the large engagement of mercenary troops.

To obtain the money for his early wars, even the silver plate from the Palace was melted down. But the inspiration of Gustavus Adolphus to his people which appealed both to their religious and patriotic senses produced a warlike attitude which swept everything before it.

Close to Gustavus Adolphus were a number of brilliant and illustrious ministers, and notable among them the Imperial Chancellor, Axel Oxenstierna.

The King had put the civil administration of the country into excellent order and he had the touch of a great man in that he was never loth to seek the advice of others, especially those whom he considered to be as independent as himself.

More than this, he was clever enough to see that the rather wayward noble families reaped direct advantages from assisting in the wars. In return he demanded that they give their services unstintingly to their country.

In the year of Christina's birth, thanks largely to Oxenstierna, the aristocratic families were given a direct interest in the government of the country by the establishment of the House of the Nobles.

At the same time, the Courts of Justice were reorganized and a Superior Court, Sve Hofratt, was established.

These demanded both time and energy from the Swedish aristocracy, but few tangible rewards.

The latter, however, were amply provided by trading companies – which began to penetrate to all parts of Europe – and trading communities, such as Gothenburg, which inaugurated Swedish traditions in international trade, shipping, and shipbuilding.

Nor had Oxenstierna forgotten the ordinary people. At the suggestion of the King, Uppsala University, the City of Eternal Youth, was expanded by the donation of Crown land. Schools, probably better than in any country except France, were established.

The rights of every Swede were safeguarded by Parliamentary Regulations which were admired even by such democratic-minded leaders as Cromwell.

By all these means, Gustavus Adolphus welded the country into the unit of steel which was able to challenge even the powerful domination of the Hapsburgs and the Catholic Union in Europe.

The cares of the warrior King soon banished the possibility that he could play the doting father for very long after Christina's birth.

Nevertheless, she was the only living person who could ever sway him from his sense of duty.

On one occasion he had travelled far to the north to inspect the Falun copper mines which he rightly realized would solve his country's economic problems far better than the acquisition of loot through the course of successful wars.

He had gone to welcome miners, smiths and craftsmen who had been invited from all over Europe to come and live in Sweden.

While he was with them, a messenger arrived from Stockholm to say that his baby was ill, one of the many occasions when Christina suffered from a form of nervous prostration which was to affect her all her life.

Immediately the King cancelled all his arrangements and rode day and night till he reached Stockholm.

He was continually and uneasily conscious of the neglect of his baby daughter by the Queen and the servants under her influence. To obviate the danger to Christina's life he took her with him whenever he could.

At first the child rode on a special pannier on a pony, then when she was a little more than a year old, on the pommel of the saddle of her father's horse.

When the King went to inspect the new fortifications of Kalmar, the fortress city which he called the Key of the Empire, he was furious because no cannon crashed out a Royal salute as his cavalcade approached.

But before he could voice his displeasure the Commandant of the fort came forward saying apologetically:

'We did not follow the custom, Sire, for fear that it might frighten the Princess.'

The King looked down at the child, who was gazing with

interest at the soldiers drawn up in front of her. Then he laughed.

'Fire the salute,' he said. 'She is a soldier's daughter and must get accustomed to it.'

The Commandant hurried back to the fortress and soon the cannon boomed the salute as usual.

It is recorded that, much to her father's delight, Christina clapped her hands with pleasure, and even though she was still unable to talk, showed by signs that she would like the noise to occur again.

Needless to say, the King was delighted at this reaction and said to his companions:

'You see, she is a Vasa. She will be as intrepid as all the Kings of Sweden.'

After this he used to take her to every review of his troops.

Thus Christina's earliest and formative years were surrounded by the panoply of martial strength.

She was taught to look on the earthy masculinity of the common soldier as a supreme virtue, to regard a display of force as the apex of human ambition. She had not feared the booming cannon, nor did she cringe when the uncouth men of Sweden's armies jostled around her.

Time after time she stood beside her father as his mobile leathern guns rumbled past, pulled either by a horse or three men.

Unlike their German enemies, she did not think that the swarthy, dwarfish Lapps, as hairy and shaggy as the ponies they rode, were some kind of animal.

She loved the fair-haired giants, Southern Swedes, who formed the crack cavalry, and she smiled impartially on the Italians, Netherlanders, Scotsmen and outlaws of a score of countries who had flocked to the Vasa banner.

The child came to know thousands of the men personally. Every soldier who fought under the command of Gustavus Adolphus was given an hymn-book, and it did not matter that only a proportion of them could read the battle songs which were printed there.

These books were symbols of the sacredness of the Swedish cause, and they were further blessed by the Royal touch of Vasa.

For half an hour at a time the infant Christina handed out book after book to the soldiers.

Sometimes a man would stand rigidly at attention, more often he would kneel and brush her hand with his mouth.

In those weeks before her father went to war she learned the deep delight that comes from the worship of men, the sense of power from the devotion of giant strength to the gentleness of a weaker sex and a weaker human being.

Perhaps deep in her psychological make-up at those military rallies another piece of the jigsaw which was the Christina of the morrow fell into place.

A woman could demand veneration; she need not be a slave of men – even to command their love.

And with the impressions of the extent and limitation of physical strength she also obtained a realization of the power of God. Her father had no doubts whatsoever that he fought under the direct guidance of God Himself.

So implicit was the King's faith in his divine destiny that he took fantastic risks with his own life. Christina loved these stories of supernatural influence.

'Tell me of the man with the leaden heart,' she would say as she rode in her father's arms after a long day with the troops.

He would laugh at her insistence because she knew the oft-told tale as well as he, but he would be serious as he began the account once again, for it was as holy to him as a tale from the Bible.

'There was an Italian among my mercenaries, a good fighter but a man of little honour. He came to my banner because we were victorious and he knew that there would be steady pay, proper victuals and care when he was sick.

'But that did not ensure his fidelity. He was an adventurer and open to bribery. My enemies approached this man secretly, knowing that any of my soldiers could come to my battle lodging at any time to speak to me. They paid him many talers to kill me.

'One evening as I finished my meal this man walked up and stood beyond the camp fire. When I looked up I saw that there was a pistol in his hand. I walked across to the foolish fellow and gently consoled him, for he was sorely troubled, weeping and distraught. I touched his pistol and demanded why it remained clenched but unfired in his hand, though primed and ready.

'"As I looked on you, Sire, there was a golden light around

you," he said. "My hand was paralyzed and it seemed as if my heart had become as lead in my breast."

'And so it was. His fingers remained rigid on the pistol, and the elbow bent. Until we prayed together he could not move a muscle.'

The story was true enough. Just as Gustavus Adolphus's ship had never succumbed in a storm, nor his horse stumbled accidentally, nor the plague stolen his life, so this assassin found himself physically incapable of the deed about which he had previously felt no qualms of conscience.

The first six years of Christina's life were full of idyllic interludes in company with her father, and possibly it was the only time that she was really happy. But such times were all too short, because Gustavus Adolphus was continually out of the country fighting his wars.

He left first for Poland when she was six months old, returning before her birthday when snow and ice made warfare impossible.

Not until May, 1629 – the twelfth year of the Thirty Years War – did he return home permanently, or that is, as permanently as was ever permitted in his reign by a temporary peace.

That autumn he signed the Truce of Altmark, but it was only a truce.

In the winter of 1629–30 preparations for war were continuing, and Christina, now three years old and constantly the companion of her father, became accustomed to an endless procession of couriers, ambassadors and generals of the Swedish army, discussing the plans for a campaign which was to prove a triumph for Sweden and a tragedy for her.

As the time came for him to lead his expeditionary forces against Germany, the King arranged to make a formal farewell to the Estates. On this occasion he took Christina with him, giving her into their protection as heir to the throne and his most beloved child.

In his soldier's uniform he looked round the great hall in which were sitting the men who represented his people, and said:

'Seeing that many may imagine that we charge ourselves with this war without cause given, so take I God the Most High to witness that I have undertaken it not out of my own pleasure nor from lust for war, but for many years have had ever present the motive thereto – mostly so that our oppressed brothers in religion may be freed from the Papal yoke, which by God's grace we hope to effect.

And since it usually comes to pass that the pitcher which is carried often to the well comes to be broken at last so will it come with me too. I who in so many trials and dangers have fought for Sweden's good and have until now escaped through the gracious protection of God with life unharmed, must lose it one day.'

There was an unusual silence in the hall and many a sidelong glance at the Astrologer who stood, as usual, not far from the King.

These people, devout Christians as they were, and ready to fight for the Christian beliefs they held, were not far removed from their mystic Viking ancestry. They took the Royal premonition as a true and ominous one.

There was no doubt that the King also believed that this might well be the last time he ever saw his people in his country's capital.

For a full minute after the King sat down there was silence. He looked at the little child who stood immobile by his side, then he rose again.

'Before I depart I commend you, all you people of Sweden both present and absent, to God the Most High. Wishing that after this life we may, by God's good pleasure, meet and consort in all that is Heavenly and eternal.'

Christina had been taught a short speech to recite, and not really understanding what her father was saying, she impatiently tugged at his coat, anxious to show that she was able to perform her Royal duty.

He looked down at her and, for the first time in his life, his iron resolution broke. He picked her up in his arms, kissing her fondly, tears rolling down his cheeks.

Then, still holding the child in his arms, he listened while the whole assembly swore allegiance to Christina. She was declared heir to the throne, and not heiress.

At this symbol that she was to be regarded as a man, the whole assembly cheered her loudly.

After this formal arrangement, Gustavus Adolphus finished more detailed preparations for the protection and education of his daughter. He put her in the care of his sister, Princess Catharine, and arranged for Catharine's husband, John Casimir, to be in charge of the Royal finances.

When Queen Eleanora heard that she was to be deprived of any influence over her child, she went into one of her hysterical outbursts, to which the King listened without comment.

It is evident from some remarks that she made during this meeting, that the King was even more alarmed than before at her unnatural attitude to her daughter.

He immediately gave orders that not only was the Queen not to be responsible for Christina's upbringing, but that she should be specifically excluded from any State business by which she could thereby gain control of the child's affairs.

In giving these orders to Oxenstierna, he excused himself by saying:

'I consider women, and unfortunately particularly this woman, to be unsuitable to hold any position in State affairs.'

Oxenstierna made no reply and concealed his feelings. He must have been slightly amused and no doubt considerably relieved that the King had arranged this delicate matter without his interference.

He ignored the paradox that in fact a woman – the King's sister – was to be a very powerful member of Christina's guardians. The actual affairs of the country Gustavus Adolphus put in the hands of the State Council, which consisted of five members acting as a Regency.

The King then turned to the question of his daughter's education. His main object was to have her brought up exactly as if she had been a boy.

'I want you to teach her everything that a Prince of Sweden should know,' he explained to Oxenstierna. 'She must learn the arts of war, and the art of civil government. She must not waste her time with embroidery, painting and similar trivialities with which women fill their time.

'I want you to make her strong, and for this she must take hard and vigorous exercises every day. She must learn how to shoot, how to fence, and how to gallop for hour after hour in all sorts of weather.

'Of course, it will be necessary that she maintains those virtues which make a woman seemly in a world of men. It will be natural that she should show modest virtue in everything she does. But these assets will not minimize her appeal as a Prince of the realm and not a Princess.'

He dismissed his Chancellor and resumed his study of military matters. Not a detail was omitted from his attention.

He dealt with the financing and feeding of his soldiers, with the forced recruitment of every man up to fifty years of age, with the strategy for his armies from the Rhine to the Oder and from Vienna to Hamburg.

When everything possible had been done, he returned to take command of his expeditionary forces.

In the spring of 1632 that perpetual tension that comes from military stalemate reached its climax in Stockholm.

The hopes that the pennants of Sweden would flutter around the walls of Vienna herself had been frustrated when Wallenstein was reappointed Commander of Austria's Imperial armies.

The talk in the Swedish War Council of coming attack turned to discussions on hurried defence to protect the Northern territories of Germany.

As soon as the early summer sunshine dried the terrain Gustavus Adolphus moved his armies by forced marches until he was over the Danube.

Every man, officers and baggage-bearers included, was ordered to help dig in near Nuremberg. Not far off, and only a few days later, Wallenstein began constructing an earth fortress so as to block the only usable highway to the North.

In the harbour at Stockholm, and along the coast in every tiny creek, ships lay laden with food. The farms had been denuded of the remaining stores of the previous autumn's harvest. Stacks of dried fish began to go bad.

The signal to sail could not be given, for the possibility of getting the supplies through to the armies did not arise.

Sweden faced near-starvation. Dumps of supplies had proved to be rotten when unloaded.

Christina learned to eat up every scrap of food because it was unpatriotic to waste it, and she was reprimanded for complaining when her meals became plain and short.

She also had another glimpse of the desolation which war and death can bring.

Hearty, swashbuckling men who had seemed to her the epitome of strength and life as they had lifted her up in their arms, the roughness of their hands and the metal of their breastplates hurting her as they held her while she watched her father review their regiments, were now mentioned as dead.

But they had died not in the glory and honour of battle but from the contemptible death of disease.

This was the enemy which struck at the half-starved Swedish army without ceasing while their mortal adversaries remained afraid.

News became fitful. A messenger arrived with information that the King, exasperated by the slow decimation of his forces by disease, starvation, and desertion, had made a frantic, hopeless sortie against the huge earthworks thrown up by Wallenstein.

The Swedish soldiers crawled like ants up the almost perpendicular slopes, and like ants they were crushed to death.

Stockholm did not know of this disaster for many days. No messenger came with the news of defeat to a man who had never seemed to know defeat. Yet there was no sense of expectant triumph in the city.

No news was bad news.

For Gustavus Adolphus had never failed to send a speedy messenger with tidings of victory, knowing that the real army was the Swedish nation herself, and that he and his soldiers were merely the tools of his people.

The summer grew. Everything seemed at peace when Christina was taken for her riding lessons in the glades of the forests around Sweden.

The cattle had calved. The blossom transformed the countryside and the pastures were vivid with flowers. Plant life burgeoned forth as the snows on the mountains receded.

With the warm weather came exciting news.

The King was on the move once more, fighting the war of movement in which he excelled. Nuremberg was in the hands of a garrison, but the main forces had gone south again, their eyes on Vienna.

They lived off the land, spreading want and destruction as they fed themselves back to strength.

The statesmen of Stockholm knew much later than Gustavus Adolphus that the manoeuvre had failed. Wallenstein was a cool and calculating adversary, ready to sacrifice much if in the long run he could gain the day.

He struck at the Swedish communications, seeking to break both tangible and political connections with the allies of Gustavus Adolphus in Saxony.

While Stockholm was dreaming of Sweden destroying a vital limb of the Catholic body at Vienna, the King was facing the nightmare of withdrawing five hundred miles to the north to prevent the disaster of a winter in a hostile and denuded Europe without commissariat connection with the homeland.

The army marched sixteen hours a day – a great serpent weaving across a terrified countryside, leaving a trail of desolation in its path.

Stragglers were set upon and murdered. The dying lay down beside the dead. Four thousand horses dropped from exhaustion.

But the army achieved the seemingly impossible and by the beginning of November, sixteen thousand men deployed outside the little town of Lutzen, some miles to the south-west of Leipzig.

A pall of smoke hung over the huddled buildings in the cold, dank air. It came from the hundreds of fires used to cook the evening meal of Wallenstein's army which had crammed Lutzen to bursting point as they prepared to settle there for the winter.

By nightfall a cold mist had blotted out the scene. In the clammy fields the Swedish men huddled together, too weary to forage for food.

The only activity was around a sullen fire of sodden branches which marked the King's headquarters. He talked to his officers resolutely, optimistically.

As he outlined his plans for attack at dawn he might have been the well-fed and well-rested man who had planned the war years before in the palace of Stockholm.

His personality was infectious. Before the King lay down and fell instantly asleep he had imbued his followers with his own implicit faith that the morrow would not be merely a day of battle, but the dawn of a great triumph.

What fate that momentous day brought to European civilization was not known for several weeks in Stockholm. Christina caught the air of tense expectancy which pervaded the palace after the brief news had arrived that Gustavus Adolphus was hurrying north.

It was long before daybreak one early December morning that the little Princess awoke and imperiously demanded that her nurse dress her and take her to the great hall of the palace whose doors gave on to the courtyard.

She did not tell the woman that she had been disturbed by a nightmare in which she saw her father fighting a dragon. The

King had disappeared into the smoke from the beast's nostrils and she had awoken in floods of tears.

The dream convinced her that there would be news that morning.

She was right. A horseman clattered into the courtyard, having ridden overland from the south of the country. Christina was at the doors of the hall, standing beside a surprised and sleepy sentry.

As he dismounted she saw that the man was Leubfling, her father's friend and personal groom.

The man's exhausted face frightened her. She backed away a little, as if to delay what she believed to be the inevitable. Then a comforting hand reached down to hers. Her Aunt Catharine had also risen early.

It was the older woman who spoke first to the mud stained messenger.

'What news do you bring of the battle?' she demanded.

'A victory for Sweden, Madam,' he said, the smile on his mouth belying the dark sorrow of his eyes. 'It is a great victory, perhaps the most wonderful the banners of the Vasas have ever blessed. The enemy has been completely routed.'

The weary man swayed as he stood. Christina drew in her breath.

'And the King – my father?' she asked in a whisper.

Leubfling turned his head aside as if he dared not look in her eyes.

'His Majesty was killed in the hour of victory,' he answered.

The Princess Catharine picked Christina up in her arms and carried her to a chair. The child was icily calm. Only her almost transparent pallor as the blood was drained from her face gave evidence of the emotional shock.

As if by some telepathic means men and women from all parts of the palace came hurrying into the hall. Menials stood beside high officials, women from the kitchens unconsciously rubbed shoulders with the nobles.

Someone thrust a tankard of hot spiced wine into Leubfling's hand.

He sipped it gratefully and because of his exhaustion sat down unrebuked on a settle by the still warm ashes of a log fire which had blazed there the previous day.

'We joined battle shortly after dawn,' he began slowly. 'As the day strengthened the mist became thicker. Everywhere was the noise of moving men, of jangling harness, of intermittent shots. As a figure loomed out of the fog one could not tell at twenty paces whether he were friend or foe.

'His Majesty bade me keep close to him – a feat I found difficult for he spurred his horse all the time to the gallop. As always he chose the right wing to lead personally. The destruction as we charged was terrible.

'The enemy had placed their best men, the Imperial Musketeers, in ditches along the road we had to cross so they could fire upwards at our horses' bellies. Volley after volley brought down our finest troopers. But God was with us, and when all was confusion the fog lifted suddenly.

'I was beside the King and we were alone but for five or six horsemen. Suddenly there was a mighty shout behind us. Our soldiers had seen their King and they charged. The enemy was forced to retire as if an avalanche had struck them!

'We were almost to the walls of burning Lutzen when the King saw that the centre of the charge, hard pressed by immeasurably superior odds, was faltering. He rode straight to his men, galloping through the enemy lines, reaching his objective before they could guess who was among them.'

Leubfling smiled proudly at the memory.

'It would not be seemly to repeat the oaths and jokes the King made to rally the troops. He knew when to curse, when to banter, when to encourage – and yes, even when to plead. But most of all he knew how to set an example. He called for a fresh horse, and one for me. When they had been brought he turned and rode at the enemy.

'It was then that God deserted him, though in His mercy He had not deserted our cause. The fog descended and my horse stumbled because he could not see the ground below his hooves. I lost sight of the King for a full five minutes. When I found him his left hand hung useless by his side, and he was controlling his horse by pressing the flanks with his knees.

'I saw the blood running down over his wrist and hand. But he took no notice. With his good right arm he was still flaying right and left with his short sword – often I dare swear, at nothing. He was a man possessed and fought the very air itself.

'I took the reins and guided his mount from the thick of the battle. I was on his left, and I curse myself for it. If I had been on the King's right my body would have welcomed the cannon-ball that crashed into his chest, almost knocking him from the saddle. I dismounted and caught him as he fell.

'Once again the fog lifted. I knew my King was dying. But the enemy was impatient. A soldier, crouching in a gully near by, fired his musket and smashed my master's face to a bloody pulp.

'Fearing more blasphemous insults to the dead I hit the King's horse across the flanks so that it should not stand there proclaiming with its purple caparison the Royal identity of its rider.

'The ghost of our King rode away on the empty saddle. I saw the horse's neck arch as if the bit had been pulled in his mouth and then gallop along our lines. Once, twice, three times the King's mount galloped from one end to the other. On its last gallop it was mad with pain from a wound in its neck.

'Our men knew that the King had died a soldier's death by that token of the riderless mount. They did not feel despair, but the desire to avenge him. There was a terrible cry of men maddened by blood lust and bereft of all sense of their own lives.

'Without spoken orders, and only at the behest of the riderless horse, they ran forward. Some were crawling along, wounded. Many were dragged by horses spurred ahead by their riders. I found a horse and joined the charge. The enemy stood up, looked, and fled.

'Such anger soon spends itself, and more slowly such terror can be mastered. It is true that for a time our onward march was halted. Then tactics replaced foolhardy bravery. The King's orders for the battle were carried out, and by nightfall Lutzen had been won.

'After darkness had fallen we sought our King. He lay naked under a heap of dead. His face we hardly recognized from the musket ball that killed him. We saw other wounds. There were three other balls embedded in his flesh; a dagger thrust in his arm near the shoulder.

'Next day we bore our King in death, as he had moved in life, in the midst of his soldiers. The cavalry preceded him; the foot-soldiers followed. Then, when I had seen my master resting in God's peace at Weissenfels, I began my journey home.'

As Leubfling finished his story, his voice broke and the

tears he had restrained so long flowed down his cheeks. And all those in the hall wept with him.

The Golden King of Sweden was dead. A world showed its grief.

In Stockholm a little girl who was now Queen endured the choking suffocation of the misery of knowing the only human being in the world she could love and trust would never again lift her on to his broad secure shoulder.

Somewhere on the way back to her hated Sweden the widowed Queen indulged in hysterical and ostentatious grief. The King's arch enemy, the Archduke Ferdinand, wept for a noble adversary. The bells tolled for a dead hero.

Gustavus Adolphus had achieved a conqueror's glory, but he had exacted a conqueror's price.

More than a million people had been killed or died from plague and starvation. As the funeral bells of Northern Europe boomed monotonously they were accompanied by the clatter of carbines where men and women, infected by rabies which followed the Swedish armies, were shot.

Rotting bodies lay unburied over half a continent, spewing out disease as unseasonable warmth fought off the cleansing cold of winter. Wolves left the forests and boldly scavenged on human flesh in farms and hamlets.

Men and women who had been born in the same year as Gustavus Adolphus, and had lived their adult lives in the perpetual degradation of the wars he had to wage, were wrinkled and aged in the month of his death, though they were but thirty-seven years old.

This was the real memorial to a mission of faith, and there were those in Sweden who saw the truth behind the panoply of victory celebrations.

It is perhaps not very strange that among them was the clear-eyed child of six years old who inherited both the blessings and the curses of her father's life.

CHAPTER THREE

THE day after the news of the battle at Lutzen reached Stockholm, the Councillors of State met in bewilderment, fear, and in some cases, with secret and disloyal ambitions.

With the death of the King the country had lost its guide and leader, and the Council lacked the wisdom of Oxenstierna.

The Chancellor had been ordered to Europe a year before. He saw the King in Frankfurt two months before Lutzen. Then he moved to Nuremberg. The news of Gustavus Adolphus's death did not reach him for a month.

He remained in Germany as supreme representative of his country, endowed with autocratic powers, but the savour had gone from his life.

'We will have eventually to conclude a peace with honour,' he told his clerk, 'and so extract the Fatherland from this interminable war. Otherwise one day we might have to run from it instead of walk with dignity.'

While Oxenstierna wrestled with the problems of his country in Germany, the members of the Swedish Government pursued their various policies, each with his own ideas of what the future should be.

Many of the new and powerful representatives of the country believed that a republic would be better than a kingdom ruled by a six-year-old child.

But Christina's many journeys with her father now stood her in good stead.

The troops wanted her as Queen; many of the nobles were convinced that a monarchy was the only system which would enable them to retain the wealth they had gained by looting in Europe, while the peasants had their traditional veneration of a person of Royal blood.

At the meeting held on the morrow of the news of the King's death, the eventual policy, after interminable argument and bickering, was to do nothing; a policy which is sometimes the best.

33

Christina, therefore, found herself moved from the position of a well-loved Princess to the cold eminence of the throne.

Servants and statesmen who had hitherto treated her with affection but courteous devotion now became remote as they bowed deferentially and addressed her in the third person.

She was bewildered and unhappy as she realized that she was bereaved not only of her father but also of any affection and love that had existed apart from him.

She was constantly being politely corrected for calling herself 'I' instead of 'we'.

She found she could neither request advice as to what to do, nor, in fact, give instructions which, because of her youth, would be carried out.

In addition, the austere Lutheran religion demanded that she wear an incongruous long black dress which impeded her movements and made her feel ugly and ungainly.

Although she was only six years old she was already acutely conscious of her appearance.

The months of winter passed slowly and miserably. Because of Court mourning there were no festivities at Christmas time, nor in the more important celebration of the New Year.

Then, on the 1st day of February 1633, the Riksdag was convened to proclaim Christina King of Sweden.

Her nurse dressed her with care. She wore with her black dress a tiny mourning veil over her face. She was then taken by the Royal coach to the Riksdag.

As she entered the great building she imperiously threw back her veil so that she could look at the men who were to decide her future.

She clambered on to the massive oaken throne which had been the seat of the Swedish Kings for generations, sitting right on the edge with her feet dangling in the air.

Yet she did not look pathetic or ridiculous. At that moment she impressed men who were still doubtful that a child should rule their country. There was only one man among them ready to voice the earlier doubts of them all. He was an uncouth representative of the peasants named Larsson.

'Who is this child?' he demanded. 'We do not know her, and I have never seen her.'

As a member of the Order of Peasants he sat with his colleagues on benches at the rear of the great hall. The child was an almost indiscernible figure in the gloom of that February morning.

The Marshal of the Diet, who was standing next to the throne, picked up Christina in his arms and carried her on his shoulder among the assembled members. Christina looked proudly around her and met the challenging gaze of Larsson with unblinking eyes.

The man examined her closely. Then he smiled and shouted:

'It is herself. She has the very eyes, nose and forehead of Gustavus. She is truly a Vasa. Let her be our Queen.'

There was a murmur of agreement which rose to a crescendo of cheers. Christina had entered the lists against the critics among her people for the first time, and her triumph was as great as any she ever had.

With this confirmation of her position, her life became far more regimented. A period of training and education began which in many ways was akin to that of an animal for a circus.

The unimaginative men appointed to direct her life lacked, with one exception, the humanity to realize that a Royal child was also a human child.

To some extent this was the fault of her father whose frantic anxiety to see that Sweden was well governed had caused him to lay down rules for her education, while omitting to make any provision for the relaxation which his own presence would have ensured.

Before he set out to lead his armies he had lectured his Councillors and Christina's future tutors.

'I believe God means my daughter to be the Champion of the Protestant Faith,' he averred. 'My father knew of my mission and he set me the example for the training of my own child. I was weaned on affairs of State; my toys were the drafts of treaties.'

This was true enough. Gustavus Adolphus had played on the flagstones of his father's Council chamber before he could walk.

He had endured the cold and filth of campaigning before he was seven, and at ten he had taken an active part in the government's deliberations. By the time he became King, when he was seventeen, he was a ruler in fact as well as in name.

Christina had learned to feel pride in her father's exploits; but she was also inculcated by gossip with a revulsion against

35

all that his campaigns of a Holy War had meant beneath the surface.

Only a child with the seeds of sadism in her heart could have endured at such a tender age the raucous talk of the hardened soldiers, only someone utterly heartless could have thought of war without bitterness when it had deprived her of the one person who gave her a sense of absolute security, the one person who had filled her young life with his love.

Many months before, she had listened while Gustavus Adolphus reiterated to a newly recruited regiment his orders for discipline:

'Under the flag of the Vasas,' he had said in his slow, deep voice, 'there shall be no rapine or pillage. If there seems no way of attack except by the destruction of hospitals and churches, and the murdering of the civil population, then know this is the Devil's work. God will show a way without such bestiality, and the men who break my rules will be punished by death.'

Amid the foreboding of tragedy that strikes every child who is brought close to the acts of ruthless men, these words of the King had perhaps during his lifetime mollified Christina's normal horror of war and all that it meant.

But after his death she heard other things which became the figments of nightmares as she lay in her large bare bedroom, lit only by the flickering torches from the courtyard below.

'The Protestant Messiah', as Maximilian of Bavaria called the Swedish King, and 'the Rising Sun', which was Richelieu's descriptive eulogy, had taken terror as well as religious freedom to the people of Europe.

Plague and bad harvests became the allies of both sides. As far away as the Tyrol people were grinding acorns and tree roots to make bread; in Poland bodies, mummified by starvation, lay unnoticed by the roadside as the troops marched by.

Gustavus Adolphus had moved to death and victory through lands turned to a living hell.

The Catholic forces burned for the fun of it; church roofs were melted down to make shot, their walls torn away to make fortifications.

Shortly before news of her father's death Christina had attended a parade of the embarking forces when an agent back from Brandenburg harangued the troops with stories of the vicious enemy they were to destroy.

36

She had heard him describe how hostages had been dragged for miles while tied to the tails of horses, how terrified burghers had written prayers on the demand lists as the only possible reply to the fantastic indemnities demanded against destruction.

She learnt of men being roasted over fires and suffocated in ovens, of goblets of urine forced down the throats of prisoners to give them a foretaste of the 'Swedish drink of alliance'; of sports where prisoners were tied in rows and wagers made on the number of victims one pistol shot could penetrate.

To the men of the Swedish armies these absolutely true tales were the tinder to a smouldering hate. They produced the needful will to wage war.

To a child of six they were merely the fiendish pattern of an adult world she was told she would one day control and direct.

The one trace of decency she had been able to hold on to was that these bestialities were the practices of the enemy. The Swedish armies were implicitly forbidden to indulge in them.

But in the days that followed the news of her father's death she realized that often the iron restraint was relaxed, either for political reasons, or because the troops were out of control.

When this happened the Swedes made up for the past by excesses which rivalled and even eclipsed those of the enemy.

Throughout her life Christina remembered the ghastly tragedy of the Maiden City of Magdeburg.

For two days in May, 1631, the city waited vainly for the arrival of Gustavus Adolphus with help for his ally, Falkenburg, who was holding out against besieging Catholics.

They broke in at mid-morning, and for a day and a night and a day the town was looted and burned. For a fortnight afterwards the wagons rumbled out with the dead – twenty-four thousand men, women and children, stabbed, raped, and burned.

Only the barrels of wine in the cellars escaped the holocaust and for days the drunken troops rolled about the still smouldering streets, kicking at the starving dogs which fought and snarled over the human corpses.

Only five thousand people out of a population of thirty thousand survived to re-erect the wooden statue of a young girl which had stood over the town gate with the words 'Who will take it?' on her wreath of virginity.

The emblem of purity and unassailability was charred and broken.

To all Protestant Europe the foulness of Magdeburg's death meant a battle cry of 'Magdeburg quarter' whenever the vanquished pleaded hopelessly for mercy. To little Christina the cry was a prolongation of the shame into which even the men around her could fall.

Wartime breeds a callous and brutal outlook. No one worried that Christina had the habit of standing silent and wide-eyed within hearing of officers and politicians who gloated over the rapine and pillage of the campaigns in Europe.

Nor did the tutors soften the psychological hurt by deprecating an evil which they may even have argued was necessary.

Although Gustavus Adolphus, so trustful of God's wisdom in directing his actions, had failed his daughter by selecting unsuitable men to educate her, it was actually very difficult for him to choose men of the right type.

All those he could count on as loyal friends were soldiers first and foremost, and culture came a long way behind.

In the absence of Oxenstierna the most important person in Christina's training was Axel Baner, Master of the Royal Household, and one of the late King's greatest friends.

He held his position largely because he was the brother of one of the best Generals in the Swedish army. He had no education whatever and had spent most of his life carousing, fighting and generally enjoying himself.

He was an enormous man of very great strength, his passion for physical exercise counteracting the excesses of his life. Christina was frankly terrified of him.

When his conscience sent him to her after weeks of neglect his booming voice would herald his approach and he would laugh boisterously and condescendingly at practically anything she said.

A second governor of the infant Queen was Gustav Horn. He was a Senator who could have been a fine guardian for Christina, for he was a man of unusual learning and breeding, but he had little love for children of any kind.

In any event most of the diplomatic work of the country fell on his shoulders and there were very few occasions indeed when he could personally supervise what was going on.

The result of the neglect of these two men was that most of Christina's education in her early years was given by

John Matthiae, who had been a Chaplain in the Swedish armies.

He had held the services before a hundred battles while the King lived, and when he was too old for campaigning, had been presented with important positions in the Swedish universities.

His influence over Christina was very great, and although the King had chosen him because of his veneration of the Lutheran religion, he did in effect sow in her mind the seeds of Roman Catholicism.

Despite Matthiae's gentleness, he was so imbued with the need to implant learning in his little ward that he planned Christina's life so that she had hardly any time whatever to herself.

She was in the schoolroom at the Palace by six o'clock in the morning, and worked without ceasing until midday. The preparation for the daily examination occupied all the afternoon, as well as the evening long after she should have been in bed.

On Saturdays, thanks to Axel Baner, she left the schoolroom, but still the discipline continued with violent physical exercises, which not only strengthened but coarsened her as well.

She was taught to shoot from the saddle, to fence and to keep her seat at full gallop over the rough countryside around Stockholm.

As it was utterly impossible for a child to expend this physical energy for more than a morning, she was allowed to 'rest' on Saturday afternoons by holding conversations in various foreign languages with her tutors.

What this curriculum did to her emotional life can only be imagined, but physically and intellectually she progressed enormously.

At the age of ten she could talk fluently in German, French and Latin, and she was already starting to learn Spanish, Italian and Greek.

Her progress was all the more remarkable because of the unnatural influence of her mother.

The Regency had done their best to carry out the King's orders and deprive Queen Eleanora of direct contact with her child, but, in view of her bereavement, it was quite impossible for them to do so all the time.

When Christina was proclaimed King in February 1633, Maria Eleanora was out of the country. She had gone to Germany to bring back her husband's body, and it was not until July that she returned to Sweden.

On that occasion Christina, once again deep in mourning, was taken by coach to the little seaport of Nyköping.

In procession with the Court and State Council and members of the Estates and nobility, she walked slowly to the quay where the coffin stood draped in black, with the widowed Queen prostrate across it.

The day was unusually hot and by the time the child reached the coffin, perspiration was running down her face and she swayed with exhaustion.

Her mother, believing that Christina was trying to keep away from her, rushed forward and threw her arms round her daughter, moaning and crying.

All the way back to Stockholm, with the funeral cortège moving at walking pace, Christina had to endure her mother's hysterical outbursts of grief.

At times she complained that the child was not showing any emotion and at others protesting that she would protect her little girl now that she had lost her father.

After this terrible day Christina was sick for some time, partly through the physical exhaustion of the experience, but also because once again she was suffering from one of those emotional crises which at intervals during her life left her prostrate.

All the time she was ill the mother sent constant messages summoning her to her room. As soon as Christina was well enough to get up she obeyed. No one had the sense to tell the child what she would see.

She was ushered from the blazing sunlit passages, to a darkened room where the only light came from two small candles.

As her eyes became accustomed to the gloom she saw that the whole room, walls, ceiling and windows, had been draped in black cloth. The bed itself was black and her mother lay in it wearing a long black veil.

Only her fluttering hands showed white against the prevailing darkness.

The widowed Queen did nothing but groan while Christina timorously advanced towards her and curtseyed. Then she pointed to a chest at the side of the bed on which stood a small gold casket.

'Look,' she said, 'there is the heart that used to beat so powerfully.'

Despite the protests of the Lutheran clergy, Maria Eleanora had insisted on having the body of her husband embalmed and the heart removed.

It was only when Christina began to scream aloud that she desisted from opening the casket and actually putting the heart in the child's hands.

This threat did, however, have the effect desired by the widowed Queen, for Christina began to cry and lament almost as loudly as her mother.

That it was from sheer terror and not from grief did not matter at all to the woman whose mind had almost given way.

Christina turned from the bed prepared to run from the room. She started back because of a movement in the shadows. She thought for a moment that she was seeing something supernatural.

In actual fact it was one of Maria Eleanora's dwarfs, who had been lying asleep there.

In the days and weeks that followed, when Christina was forced to obey her mother's commands and enter that terrible room for a session of perverted sentimental mourning and praying, there was always a dwarf, an imbecile or some crippled travesty of a human being for her to meet there.

This was her mother's idea of amusing herself and her child.

Suddenly in the midst of a moaning dirge for the dead King, the woman in the bed would screech:

'Now come and play with the dwarf. He is very strong and very entertaining. He is the only friend I have in the world.'

The whole Palace was, of course, aware of what was going on, and eventually they considered that the mourning period must be terminated. There were many hysterical outbursts from that funereal room, but at last the authorities got their way.

The body of Gustavus Adolphus, still awaiting burial, was taken to the great church in Stockholm and interred with the heart from the golden casket.

The day before was the last occasion that Maria Eleanora

was able to indulge in her delight for parading her grief and the last time that she was permitted to damage her daughter's mind by that travesty of amusement with her dwarfs.

As soon as the funeral was over the State Council went in formal procession to her room and informed her that on the late King's orders she was no longer to see her child.

'I do not believe it,' she stormed. 'I have lost my husband to this accursed country, am I now to lose my only child?'

In reply a letter addressed to Oxenstierna was given into her hand. Moving to the light of the candle by the empty golden casket, she recognized her husband's writing. It was a brief note and said simply:

'It is my command that you are never to permit the Queen, Maria Eleanora, to take part in the government nor in the plans for my daughter's education.'

The Royal widow raved, cried and tried to tear the letter in pieces before it was grabbed away from her. Presently she realized that she was raving in vain. The room was empty. The Council had left her.

Afterwards mother and daughter met only occasionally at formal dinner parties, or when by coincidence they walked at the same time in the Royal Park.

For Christina, life became much happier as a result of this belated decision of the Council.

For most of the time she lived in the apartments provided for her Aunt Catharine, and she never knew how difficult in consequence her aunt's life became.

By strict Court etiquette, the Dowager Queen was able to issue commands to Catharine, and they had to be obeyed.

Very often she ordered the Princess to return to her own home at Stekeborg, about twenty miles from the capital. There was nothing that the Princess could do but go, and then contrive that the Council should order her back again.

On these occasions Christina wandered around the Palace unhappy and lonely. She hardly knew where she went, except that she did her best to avoid her mother.

Not until Oxenstierna returned to Sweden in 1636 was Princess Catharine's postion regularized.

Then she was permitted to live permanently in the Palace and given authority to ignore the inevitable orders of dismissal from the Dowager Queen.

It was Axel Oxenstierna who belatedly reinforced in Christina's mind the unquestioning realization that her father had been a great hero.

He had the gift of many wise and old men of treating even an infant as worthy of serious regard and as capable as an adult of grasping the truths of emotion, thought and action.

Standing beside Christina as he always did though she had often begged that he should sit down and let her clamber on his knee, he said one day,

'We who are of Swedish blood know beyond all doubt the greatness of our King.'

Actually he talked to himself as much as to her, savouring the joy the memories of his good friend brought to him.

'In the King's service were many soldiers who came from England and Scotland,' he went on. 'Do you remember that day when His Majesty took you to the Royal docks to see some foreign soldiers embark?'

Christina nodded.

'They carried short daggers, and the jewels on them flashed in the sun.'

'Those pretty little ornaments were the terrible weapons of the men from Scotland,' the Chancellor smiled. 'Your father had many of such soldiers in his service. They formed his famous Green Brigade which brought honour to its name at Breitenfeld.

'Afterwards I met one of their leaders. He was a strange man, hot-tempered, serious about war, yet a boy in the pranks he played when in liquor. His name was Robert Monro. He boasted that in that battle he had killed a hundred Catholics.'

'These Scotsmen take no prisoners?' Christina asked severely, and with a seriousness beyond her years.

'It is said that in their own land they look on a prisoner as an enemy who may escape to fight again,' Oxenstierna replied. 'A dead enemy is an enemy no more. Yet this Colonel Monro was a man of many parts. He read to me some of his accounts of the German wars and the many monarchs for whom he has carried arms. He called your father the "King of Captains" and the "Captain of Kings".

'He told how our noble King would walk on foot within a lance throw of the enemy's cannon, oblivious of the fireballs, and then return to his officers with exact details of the enemy's strength.

'I remember how the Scotsmen admired His Majesty's

43

laughing excuses when some of his companions would remonstrate with him for risking his country and himself in actions he would never ask the youngest peasant soldier to undertake, and then lay about the pate of his cook because his dinner was late.'

Oxenstierna was silent for a time.

Forgetful momentarily of his decorum he stroked the head of the child who alone brought the image of his beloved master back to life for him.

'In all the world there was not his equal among kings,' he murmured.

He knelt down, the greatest statesman of his country and his age, helpless now to achieve his ambitions except by the humility of supplication to a tiny girl.

'Your father was my greatest friend, his army's finest general, our country's unsurpassable ruler. Through him you are growing up close to God in the faith of the Protestants. Because of his peerless understanding there are men in the college at Uppsala who can let their minds range freely without the fear of a charge of heresy – men who are your tutors.

'He has bequeathed to us a great Empire with a heart that beats steadfastly and without the agony of internal schism. All this he has done for you and for me.

'Yet in his death he has peradventure bestowed on Sweden his greatest gift: he died that we might retain the religion which we follow, he has become a martyr whose example is always before us.'

Christina, listening decorously to the old man's passionate words, possibly understood but little of what he said. But the final sentence was registered in her brain for ever.

Martyrdom was the virtue by which she finally remembered her father; martyrdom was to be the lodestar to which she was attracted for the rest of her life.

Significantly, after Oxenstierna had left her, she wandered through the palace until she found a picture hanging in an ante-room to the dead King's apartments, which were still left exactly as they were in his lifetime.

It showed a girl gazing at the Tiber from a bridge in Rome. Christina knew that Holy Bridget had been a great woman, but she did not know why.

One of her nurses, a woman who had been authorized to tend Christina despite a background which indicated a rather dangerous loyalty to Queen Maria Eleanora, came in search of her.

The nurse was old, and she remembered well the year when the house of Vasa was not the focus of loyalty that Gustavus Adolphus had made it. She was one of the many of the older generation who were perplexed and worried that the Catholic religion had become a criminal belief.

When Christina asked to know more about Holy Bridget the woman was glad to tell all she knew, for she often prayed in secret to the saint who, nearly three hundred years earlier, had lived in the glorious light of piety as the Bride of Christ and the Saviour's mouthpiece on earth.

'The blessed Bridget, like you, my little darling,' she began as she prepared Christina for bed, 'was of noble family. The Folkungs had ruled our land for a hundred years. You will hear in our sagas many stories of their strength and courage. But Bridget was gentle, kind, and pious.

'In the manner of those days she was married when she was thirteen to a youth whose parents were close friends of her father. She was not free of him until she was forty years of age.

'It was then that she received a direct revelation from God. For twenty-five years she had been living in the holy city of Rome and so, of course, God had been very near to her.'

'They say God is everywhere,' Christina interrupted.

'That is true,' the nurse agreed. 'But nowhere can we feel Him closer than in the city where the relics of His dear Son have been preserved. That is natural and right.

'We are told that the luxury and power which our Holy Father—' she corrected herself— 'which the Pope and his Cardinals have taken to themselves is the devil's work. Perhaps that is true also, for our Saviour lived in poor simplicity. But it cannot be gainsaid that Rome is the holy city . . .'

'About St. Bridget,' Christina interrupted, weary of the old woman's ramblings into religious theory.

'Yes – yes,' the nurse said, quickly conscious that her talk had been running in dangerous channels. 'In a vision the Saint was told to found monasteries and convents for the worship of God and the better understanding of His commands. Her kinsman King Magnus broke his word to give her money for this purpose. But the wrath of God voiced through Bridget was terrible.

'King Magnus tried to ignore her prophecies and refused to

45

mend his ways. Soon the Lords of Sweden revolted against him, and the Kings of Norway and Denmark rose to punish him. He was taken prisoner and passed six terrible years in dungeons.

'Even after Holy Bridget's death her vengeance lived on, and Magnus was drowned a year after she herself was taken to Heaven. She died close to God in Rome itself, but her spirit returned to our country. You have been to Vadstena?'

Christina nodded.

'Yes, my father took me to see the castle he was building there. Some women came forward and gave me a pretty lace collar.'

'The art of lace-making was bequeathed to the city by the nuns,' the nurse told her. 'They say no matter what happens this beautiful proof of the convent's existence will continue for a thousand years to come. But it is strange that His Majesty did not explain this, and a pity that he did not take you to see the blessed bones of the Saint herself, instead of showing you nothing but soldiers and cannon.'

'The bones are at Vadstena?' the child asked avidly.

'With those of her daughter, Katarina. They rest in the first of the convents built beside Lake Vattern at Vadstena. Perhaps one day you will be old enough to go and see them. I cannot read or write, but it is said that the convent became a centre where books were collected and manuscripts painted. But most of all the nuns glorified God in the way that had been revealed to Bridget.'

'Yet she did not know that it all came true,' Christina sighed. 'Because she was dead.'

'That is not true,' the nurse contradicted. 'Long after she had gone to God the blessed Saint was seen by many monks and nuns, walking serenely through the building. Yes, she knew! Of that you may be sure. And such was her power after her death, that convents were built all over the world.

'The wickedness of men has since destroyed many of them, but they spring up again. They say that the finest was in far-off England at a place called Syon. The Protestant Kings and the Virgin Queen Elizabeth forbade it to be used, and thought to put an end to its very existence.

'But they were wrong. The monks and nuns took ship to Portugal and there to this day it flourishes to the glory of God.'

'If the picture in my father's room is to be believed Saint Bridget was not a beautiful woman,' said Christina critically.

'Perhaps in the eyes of men that is so,' the nurse agreed, 'but she had a beauty of the spirit. All who came near her fell under her thrall. She was a queen over men, and never their slave as is the cunning way of those who pretend to adore a woman only to gain mastery over her body through her heart.'

She brushed the child's coarse and untidy hair and felt secretly triumphant that because of the story of Bridget her little ward had not insisted on plunging her face into cold water with that peculiar mania for cleanliness which she had shown since she was a little more than a year old.

'Now say your prayers and get you to bed,' she ordered.

Christina knelt down. For months there had been stormy tears over the question of reciting her conversations with God aloud. She insisted on thinking her words, and the evening prayer was as a result unpredictable in length.

Tonight it was long. Christina had found an interpreter.

She spoke her thoughts, not to God, but to the holy woman of Sweden whose power had spread across the world, not through the arms of metal and the bleeding bodies of mercenary troops, but through the seeping flood of religion, literature and music.

A mile away old Oxenstierna sat nodding by the fire in his home.

The State papers jumbled on a table by his side were forgotten and ignored while he pondered over his talks with a child in whom all his hopes were centred.

He had no qualms that the tiny body and childish brain were unequal to the challenge he had tried to present to them, or to the victories he envisaged in the future, for he was convinced that in a Vasa there lay the divine right to rule.

Yet had he but known it, he had that very evening lost the last battle, defeated by the half-understood rambling storytales of an illiterate nurse.

CHAPTER FOUR

As Christina entered her teens, she showed that she intended to rule in fact as well as to be Queen in name.

She studied all the war reports, and Oxenstierna found it disturbing when he arrived at the Palace to discover her sitting at her writing-table with the messages that had come in since the previous day already open and studied.

She was still very lonely.

Her mother had gone off in a pique to brood and wail over her lot in the Vasa castle at Gripsholm. This massive building set against a lake was still only partially completed since reconstruction had begun nearly one hundred years earlier.

Christina's sense of filial duty took her there at regular intervals, for even though she feared her mother, she still yearned to find some ground for mutual affection.

The visits were futile, because all that happened on each occasion was that Maria Eleanora burst into a tirade about her imprisonment.

Actually, she had gone to Gripsholm because it enabled her to exclude almost all the Swedes from her entourage and maintain a little Brandenburg Court around her.

She forgot this advantage when she grumbled and whined to her daughter.

Because Gripsholm had for centuries been used as a Royal prison in which to keep defeated monarchs and dangerous aspirants to the throne out of harm's way, she refused to speak of her home as anything but a jail.

Christina's visits to Gripsholm became more frequent after her Aunt Catharine died in 1639, and she lost the only person to whom she could open her heart. It was at this time that she began to develop emotionally.

The normal regard of one sex for the other was both mystifying and fascinating to her.

The problems of love coloured even her thoughts about politics, and many of her relatives and tutors thought it strange that a girl of thirteen should write essays and letters in such a manner.

Typical of the manner in which her mind worked as puberty brought profound mental disturbances was a note she penned to her uncle after the death of Bernard Weimar left the little duchy of Brisach without a ruler. She began:

'Most Serene and Illustrious Prince, and Dear Cousin,—I received from your lovingness two letters yesterday, to which I think it worth while to send an answer. I understand from ordinary letters that the Count Palatine is to take Weimar's army (an excellent plan).

'Mr. Treasurer wrote to me yesterday, and told me amongst other things this – in a word, that Brisach has many lovers. Kings and princes are quite mad for love of her; the King of England wants her to be set aside not for himself, but his nephews and the late Frederic's sons, and to that end has handed over large sums to the officers of Weimar's army.

'The French king is promising them likewise mountains of gold, provided they give him Brisach, who like a bride has lured them all on to love her, so that it is doubtful which of all these rival princes will enjoy the nuptial couch. I couldn't refrain from letting your lovingness know this, to let you see how fond they all are of that city.'

Like any girl of her age, Christina needed at this time the advice and instruction of an older woman.

This, unfortunately, had been an omission on the part of her Aunt Catharine, who had delayed talking to her about sex, first because Christina was too young, and then owing to the illness which preceded her death.

One day Christina went to Gripsholm determined to break down the barrier between her mother and herself.

She intended to confess that while she was beginning to feel in her body the emotional changes of an adolescent, she was overcome by the feeling of revulsion at being the slave and chattel of any man.

All her plans, however, came to nothing, because when she arrived her mother's personal equerry forbade her to disturb Maria Eleonora.

'Her Majesty is keeping a fast and has locked herself in her room with orders that she shall not be disturbed. Only the simplest food is taken to her and has to be left outside her door.

She has been in prayer and contemplation for the last five days.'

Christina was nonplussed.

Although in her own Palace in Stockholm she never brooked any interference with her desires, the whole atmosphere at Gripsholm was so redolent of her mother's presence that she turned away disconsolately and went back by boat across the lake to where her coach was waiting.

This happened on 28 July, 1640, and had she but known it, her mother was not praying in that room, but was making careful plans to leave the country.

On the following night, Maria Eleanora crept out of her room, slipped past the guards without disturbing them, and entered a carriage which was waiting to take her to Norrköping.

There she boarded a small Danish fishing vessel which sailed immediately to the Island of Gotland.

Her scheme had been organized with great efficiency and care, and after an hour's wait, she was escorted to a Danish battleship which sailed immediately for Denmark.

The ageing King of Denmark, who was no friend of the Swedish nation, had a most affectionate regard for Maria Eleanora. But her presence in his Court soon destroyed any amorous feelings he may have had for her.

Not long afterwards he was glad to get rid of her by pointing out how much happier she would be if she were back in her own country of Brandenburg.

His motive in expelling Maria Eleanora was partly personal, but he was also impelled virtually to drive her out because of the hostile attitude of Sweden.

When the Queen's flight was reported in Stockholm, Oxenstierna voiced the feelings of the whole nation when he claimed that Christian of Denmark had usurped the privileges of a friendly nation by arranging the Queen Mother's flight.

Sharp notes were sent to Copenhagen and secret orders were dispatched to the Swedish armies in Europe to prepare for war.

In fact, Maria Eleanora's flight from Gripsholm sowed the seeds for the hostilities which broke out three years later.

Christina was not so much angry as perplexed by her mother's action, and she suffered from a guilt complex that in some way she herself was to blame.

She did her best to soften the revengeful blows which the Swedish Government prepared.

A law was passed depriving Maria Eleanora of all her property in Sweden, and the churches forbade her name to be included in the prayers for the Royal Family.

Christina did not worry much about the prayers, but she did ensure that some of the revenues should be restored to her mother, and she also sent her money from her own personal income.

The shock of her failure to bridge the gulf between herself and her mother took its toll.

Shortly after Christmas, when war seemed very near and her mother was still doing her best to foment trouble in Denmark, Christina collapsed one morning during her studies, lying rigid on the floor and seemingly unconscious of everything around her.

She suffered a nervous breakdown and for many weeks walked about like an automaton.

On her recovery a new and colder Christina emerged. Oxenstierna found that she was no longer a little girl who admired him and asked his advice on any point that she did not understand, but a Queen more shrewd than her years justified.

The Regency took the wise course and gave her fuller powers.

She was admitted to all meetings of the Council, where she never sat as a silent observer, but argued constantly with the members with a cogency and common sense that disturbed them.

In particular her hostility to Oxenstierna increased.

The Chancellor had built up his career, his influence and his enormous wealth on the proceeds of war. He could, as a matter of fact, show that the financial economy of the country had been improved by the revenues and loot from the conquered countries.

But his mind was inflexible after so many years of continual strife, and he could not see that while the tangible evidence of money and land had given only a superficial appearance of wealth.

The real resources of the nation were being bled away by the drain of its man-power and the almost complete centralization of its industries for war purposes.

Christina could not forget the horrors of the atrocities,

looting and desolation, which were by now the chief evidence of the activities of the Swedish armies.

'I believe that my father, even though he was a great soldier and believed in the holiness of his cause, would wish this thing to be done with,' she said. 'Our country is not in itself a rich one, and we cannot maintain for ever one of the biggest armies in the world nor allow our consciences to condone the miseries it creates.

'Certainly it is not my wish that when I reach my majority, I should ascend a throne which is bathed in blood and supported by the harvest of death.

'I intend to travel through my Kingdom and see for myself if the poverty I hear about is a greater factor of our life than the rich palaces of my statesmen in this capital.'

While she spoke she stared unblinkingly at the old Chancellor. He showed his frowning displeasure at criticism which he had never before known even from a Vasa, but even so, this man of iron was unable to return her challenging glance.

He knew, well enough, that a new generation was beginning to think in much the same way as this exasperating but lovable chit of a girl.

He recalled the reports that had been placed on his desk that very morning. One gave the total men of conscription age in one of the Northern provincial districts.

The figure – 15,000 – was supplied by the clergy and was absolutely reliable.

The other document reported the conscripts enrolled – a mere 7,000.

No longer did the young men clamour to fight in 'The Royal Swedish War on German Soil', for the glory of God and of Sweden.

Only among the nobles and landowners, the statesmen and generals, did the war fervour remain – giving an artificial picture in Stockholm and particularly in the Palace.

The interminable preoccupation of everyone around Christina with the war developments disgusted her.

The constant alternation between disaster and triumph, with its accompanying pessimism and optimism, strengthened her loathing for the whole business.

The crushing defeat of the Swedish forces at Nördlingen in Bavaria had not, of course, been of much significance to her as she was not quite eight years old at the time.

But in the years that followed the word became a burden to her – 'Nördlingen must be avenged', 'the tactical failure of Nördlingen has been overcome', and so on, were comments she came to hate.

When Oxenstierna returned to take over the reins of government in 1636 everyone believed that conditions would quickly improve, and the magic name of Richelieu, now the friend and ally of Sweden, was bruited around as the solution of all problems.

With the simplicity of a child, Christina could not understand why the adulation of the French soon changed.

The lilies of France, she learned, were dangerous flowers. French gold and French fighting strength took the Bourbon influence over the Rhine, and left no room for the banners of the Vasas.

'We shall sue for peace,' her Aunt Catharine had told her one day when, to the consternation of the Swedish government, a courier came with the news that France had occupied Alsace. 'It would be your father's wish. The Council will surely see the advantages for ending this war before all is lost.'

Some of the Council, like thousands of ordinary people in the country, began to pray for peace.

But the nobles and the adventurers still believed whole-heartedly in the rewards of war, even if they no longer had faith in the crusading nature of their cause.

Field Marshal Johan Baner blithely ignored the more pacificatory suggestions which came sporadically from the Swedish capital to his field headquarters in Germany. War was his life, booty his income – a million talers' worth.

A brave man and a brilliant general, Johan Baner represented an age that was dying just as the child who took the details of his exploits so cruelly to heart represented the new.

For a time Baner's ambitious and unscrupulous campaigns brought him success.

The ragged, blood-drunk Swedish and mercenary armies ranged over the groaning lands of Northern and Southern Germany, their cannon thundering at the crumbling fortresses, the troops pillaging the dying towns.

Baner became the new hero of the Swedish people. When Christina walked abroad in the streets of Stockholm the people shouted his name, thinking to please the Queen by this acclamation.

It gave her a feeling of personal outrage that she should, by the trick of fortune that made her the living symbol of Sweden, be connected with a man whose reports invariably gave her a sense of foreboding.

When in 1639 Baner invaded Bohemia and besieged Prague, he justifiably explained his failure to capture the entire country by blaming the lack of food to steal and the sullen defiance of starving peasants.

Oxenstierna, in telling Christina about the matter, quoted his letter.

'I had not thought to find the kingdom of Bohemia so lean, wasted and spoiled. Between Vienna and Prague all is razed to the ground and hardly a living soul to be seen in the land.'

The imaginative Christina saw in that description no conquering army, but only the dark caparison of death. Her eyes grew moist with tears, though none fell, for she had not the God-given balm of relieving her misery with weeping.

There was one facet in Baner's character which made it possible for the little Queen sometimes to admire him.

Time after time, when Oxenstierna recounted to her the details of the newest report, she would interrupt with the query:

'And what of Mistress Elizabeth? She is well?'

Elizabeth was the devoted and long-suffering wife of the General. Perhaps because like Christina she was appalled by the agony of war, she accompanied her husband on most of his campaigns.

She served Sweden well by restraining Baner from the worst of his drinking excesses which invariably followed a day's campaigning, and she was able by a mixture of determination and gentleness to gain some control over his troops when they were let loose in a captured city.

Hard-bitten cavalrymen, roystering Scots soldiers of fortune, brutalized mercenaries from Prussia – all called her 'mother' and accepted her reprimands.

Hundreds of terrified hostages, quaking town officials, and wounded enemy prisoners had reason to bless her name, for she alone had the power to interfere with her husband's merciless demands and brutal punishment.

When Elizabeth Baner died in 1640 Christina was still in mourning for her Aunt Catharine. The one had been a real and close protector; the other was a distant and idealized ally.

Her feeling of deprivation was as great when she heard of Elizabeth Baner's death as in the loss of her aunt.

It was perhaps greater, for Christina was a Vasa and she believed implicitly that every evil action, as well as every fine and courteous one, taken in the name of Sweden was in some manner an action taken by herself.

Elizabeth Baner had been a star of virtue and mercy shining among the bloody holocaust of Swedish military manoeuvre. A tiny light had gone out on the gloomy battlefields of Europe and Christina's soul was the heavier for it.

John Baner's devotion to his wife had been a byword.

Yet at her funeral he deliberately flirted with the young daughter of the Margrave of Baden. Within a few weeks he was married to her, and as a result the thin veil of restraint which had held him back from complete degeneracy and debauchery disappeared.

His officers reported to Stockholm with exasperation that the bridal couple spent three-quarters of every night carousing and quarrelling with their friends and three-quarters of every day in the nuptial bed.

Before Baner died a few months later, in May 1641, he had brought his army down to a mutinous rabble, unpaid and unfed.

Christina was asked by the ever-optimistic Oxenstierna to give a Royal message to the troops through the man selected to succeed Baner.

He reminded her that she had met Lennart Torstensson on several occasions in company with her father, who had personally selected him as a promising officer.

The Queen could not identify Torstensson in her vague memories of those infant years, but conjured up for herself the image of a man of martial bearing, perhaps with the bright intelligent eyes which had lifted one or two of her father's friends from the brutal appearance of the ordinary fighting man.

Torstensson came to kiss her hand on the following day. He was not at all as the Queen had imagined.

The gout which eventually made it necessary for him to be carried into battle was already affecting his gait and his temper. His voice was harsh, and his manner direct.

'Men and money are the allies of victory,' he said. 'With them Your Majesty's armies can still achieve success. I shall take both with me to Germany.'

Christina dutifully wished him God-speed and said that she would pray for him and his men. Torstensson acknowledged the promise with the slightest of bows and stumped out of the audience room.

He kept his promises to the Queen and to himself.

The economic barrel was scraped to provide him with enough money to satisfy the worst grumblings of the troops, and further orders to the nobles produced another seven thousand conscripts from their estates.

In November, 1641, he took over command and brought a semblance of discipline into his forces.

The money he brought with him was paid out immediately, and thereafter he inferred that the troops must fend for themselves. In effect he legalized the pillaging which other generals had condoned.

This was the only privilege his men had. Any infringements of his rules of discipline were punished by flogging or death.

In the fierce fires of his ferocity he refashioned a fighting army as resilient as steel. As soon as the winter's snows had gone he advanced at the head of his forces, carried in his litter, and glaring around him all the time.

Vienna was his goal and he allowed nothing to stand in his way. Once more came a period of dispatches from the front bringing details of victory. They were boastful reports of the kind Christina remembered to the exclusion of all others.

There were stories of new banners waving beside the proud pennants of the Vasas – sacred vestments and altar cloths looted from Catholic churches; of tombs broken open in monasteries and rings torn from the mouldering flesh of dead monks' fingers; of the sick and aged being driven from towns where fortifications were built because they were useless; of villages and farms burned to the ground just as a warning to others not to show resistance.

With such horrors on her conscience it is small wonder that Christina did not remember to make the usual formal congratulation to her Ministers when she was told of the great victory at Leipzig, just a year after Torstensson had taken over command.

The Archduke Ferdinand himself was in charge of the

opposing forces. The Swedes outclassed him, and turned the day into a débâcle for the Imperial forces.

Five thousand men were killed; four thousand five hundred came over to the Swedish side or were taken prisoner.

Such dagger thrusts as these drained away the life-blood of the stricken body of the ancient and glorious Holy Roman Empire.

It would have been a gesture of Divine mercy if earthquake or holocaust had brought the oblivion of sudden death. But a long life made it tenacious.

The Swedish–Danish war relieved for a flash of time the death-throes at Vienna. But the rumbustious old general in the litter knew how to achieve the impossible.

In less than a year and a half he raged over the face of Central Europe, moving from Moravia to Holstein where he swept the Danes aside as if they were annoying insects and then immediately turned south in a challenge to the Austrian army.

They met near Prague. The terrible cry of 'Magdeburg Quarter' rose from the throats of thousands of soldiers whose memory turned them into Crusaders that day. The Austrian army was annihilated. Vienna lay helpless within but a few days' transport for the Swedish cannon.

But, quite suddenly, the martial force was spent – not only the strength and fighting spirit of the conquering Protestants, but the bellicose mentality of an entire continent disappeared.

The dogs of war were satisfied. Indeed, wearied and lethargic, they were back whence they had started, in Vienna. For thirty years they had ranged a continent.

Behind them, moving through the desolation, came the new aristocrats: the officers who had grown rich on pillage and political rewards, the usurers who had grown even richer from financing the merchants of death.

Now, a long way after, the statesmen gathered to wrest what they could from the shambles.

The Thirty Years War was over, although three years were to pass before the Treaty of Westphalia marked the formality of agreement.

All this time Christina had been searching for some anodyne for her bewilderment and foreboding.

The search ended in the darker avenues of sexual experimentation.

CHAPTER FIVE

EVER since her father rode out of her life when she was four years old Christina had fought off the menacing bogy of loneliness.

Children of her own age were her intellectual inferiors. This factor provoked her more than their caution in their dealings with a friend who they were told was by birth and circumstances far above them.

'Don't you dare to hit Christina; remember she's your Queen,' a well-meaning nurse had said one day.

She had come across little Charles Gustavus vigorously defending himself as Christina had tried to pull him off the riding pony.

The boy desisted immediately – and thereby won. Christina no longer wanted to ride.

More than a match for her short, rather sullen cousin, she often teased him, spurring him at long length into a physical retaliation, which gave her, as she had wished, the chance to prove her superior strength.

Incidents like this taught her that she could not choose her enemies any more than she could choose her friends.

When she was deprived of her nurse, and then, because of her advancing years, of her governess, the last defences against the misery of solitary confinement on a charge of being born a Princess crumbled.

The governess was dismissed – and left without anything more than a formal leave-taking bereft of any real affection. A companion was put in her place.

Christina paced nervously up and down her drawing-room on the afternoon that Ebba Sparre was due to be presented to her. She wished fervently to greet the girl effusively, but she knew that it was neither her nature nor place to do so.

Equally she wanted to avoid the usual formality of meeting, with the visitor standing while she sat.

She contrived it so that the visitor was announced while she was replacing some books on a shelf. The subterfuge enabled her to put the books down and then to walk across to the girl.

Ebba, the same age as Christina, stood in the doorway, neither frightened nor excited. She was too stupid to worry overmuch about her appointment. A Countess by birth, she thought the world was there merely to provide her with a living.

Most of the recent homilies on her future behaviour she had ignored.

The main point was that being a companion to a Queen would produce plenty to eat, many amusing entertainments, and with any luck, a life of comparative indolence.

It would in any event permit her to live in Stockholm, instead of in the country, which she hated.

As Christina stared at Ebba she realized that her new companion still stood by the door.

'Please come in,' she smiled reassuringly. 'I am so glad to welcome you to my home – which now will also be yours.'

She took both Ebba's hands in her own and led her to a bench by the fire. Ebba had managed nothing but a faint giggle in reply to her greeting.

The carefully rehearsed promise of devotion and the recitation of her thanks for the honour done to her had been forgotten.

She gazed at Christina with undisguised curiosity, noting the coarse quality of her clothes and the untidy manner in which they were worn.

She gaped with amazement at the muddy, heavy shoes which were exposed by Christina's gawky posture as she sprawled on the bench.

Her lips parted in a smile of irrepressible amusement which Christina preferred to regard as a token of her pleasure at being there.

For a time the girls were silent. They made a remarkable contrast.

Christina, the darkness of her skin accentuated by the tan of wind and sun, was slim even if she was dumpy. Ebba was plump and far more mature of figure than was normal at her age in these northern latitudes.

Her eyes were so large and lovely that even a member of her own sex did not at first see the vacant stupidity in them.

Her lips were full and rounded – too large perhaps for her weak chin, but so red and inviting that it hardly mattered. She was very proud of her hair – light-golden and as fine as silk.

She delighted to sit for an hour at a time brushing it, the rhythm of the movement and the sweep of the brush inducing a mental lethargy which was not far off a trance.

'You are beautiful!' Christina whispered suddenly. 'I shall call you Belle.'

'Belle?' questioned Ebba, mystified.

'You don't know French, then. It means lovely. In the Court of the King of France to call a woman "belle" is both a compliment and a term of endearment.'

Ebba mouthed the word, and liked it.

She began to smile with pleasure, and the smile lighted up her face, transforming the almost bovine stupidity with all the radiance of young womanhood. She began talking about her favourite subject – herself.

Her conversation was full of inanities and semi-lies; of imagined romances, of alleged dangers from infatuated peasant boys on her parents' estates, of illicit affairs taking place at Court.

A hundred men and women with the right to talk informally with the Queen could have chattered away in the same manner. They had never done so.

It was not a Puritan streak in her character that made Christina appear bored and impatient with ill-natured gossip. She enjoyed a vulgar or bawdy story.

The facts of life she had learned at a very early age through the coarse joking of the half-drunk nobles and officers when she had sat in banqueting halls with her father on his visits to his army and provincial officials.

In their cups no one had troubled to note that the infant Christina was listening avidly to their tales. On her return to the palace she would ask her nurse the meaning of words she had not understood, and later on the point of some of the jests.

The nurse was not particularly shocked at the child's questions. She regarded humour as being either coarse or cruel, or both. She included sexual matters as an important ingredient of such humour.

She explained the point to her little ward, and Christina, being anxious to please, got into the habit of repeating the stories she heard for the woman's amusement.

The only half-hearted reprimand she received was for the use of words more suitable for the barrack hut than a Royal Palace. Even then she was told the meaning of the word to point the moral to the veto on using it.

Now she heard for the first time the feminine version of this lewd humour. She was a little nauseated by Ebba's gentle lasciviousness, but she also found it fascinating.

On that afternoon she perhaps envied her companion's empty-headedness and wondered if the knowledge crammed in her own brain was, after all, such a valuable asset. Yet if she envied Ebba she also liked her.

They parted for the evening meal. Christina had to dine with some Councillors from Finland.

During the meal, when she ate little herself and felt that little choking her as the Finns noisily gnawed at their roast pork and drank more than was good for them, her thoughts flew constantly to Belle.

She got away as soon as she could. A candle burned on the dressing-table in the bedroom adjoining hers, which had been prepared for her companion. Ebba was passing the time by brushing her hair.

Christina stole in without being heard or seen. She stood in the shadows by the bed curtains watching.

Unconsciously her hand went to her own hair, stiff and coarse beneath her fingers. A laugh, or perhaps a sob, escaped her, and Ebba turned in alarm.

'It's only me, Belle,' Christina said, moving into the light. 'Please go on; I like watching you.'

Ebba resumed her brushing.

'It was at the midsummer fires last year,' she said softly, 'that I played the part of a Viking. My father's headman, who organized the celebrations, said that I was the only girl whose tresses were long and silky enough to be the Norse goddess.'

Christina moved a little away.

'The pagan festivals are idolatrous,' she said severely, and then as if to compensate for her criticism, 'but I suppose you cherish and care for your hair because it makes you attractive?'

Ebba turned in surprise.

'But, of course,' she answered. 'What else? A woman must be attractive to men.'

'I don't believe that.'

Again the vehemence; again the despairing challenge of the accepted role for a woman.

Ebba sensed that she had gone too far.

'But you are a Queen, and can order men to your bidding,' she suggested. 'For other girls men must be tempted into love – and marriage.'

'I'm tired,' Christina said suddenly. 'Perhaps to-night I will not summon my maids but prepare myself for rest.'

She crossed to the door, leaving it ajar.

Ebba resumed her interminable brushing. She was piqued by Christina's remark, for she had looked forward to being waited on by servants whom she could order to obey her commands.

Even she had the sense to realize that if the Queen undressed herself there would be no waiting-maids to attend the Queen's companion.

But by the time she was lying in the big uncomfortable and stifling bed her good temper had been restored. She felt she was going to like her post.

The ugly girl who was her Queen seemed more like an inferior. Ebba felt the pleasant glow known only to women, which comes from a realization of the peerless power of beauty.

Whatever rank a man's world gave the girl who had just called out 'Good night, dear Belle' from the adjoining room, she knew that in women's hearts, and most of all in the Queen's, the beauty of her body made her the mistress.

In the other room, with the bed curtains undrawn, Christina lay wide-awake, half-fearing and half-revelling in the way her mind drifted to Ebba's moonish face and placid eyes.

No matter how she tried to force her brain to repeat Latin verbs, to enumerate the principal towns of her kingdom, and to recite her prayers, there was only Ebba – and again Ebba.

Christina, moving tardily through adolescence, was in love.

She dreamed that night – dreams of girls and women who had registered in her subconscious although ignored by her conscious mind.

A young fisher girl, her bosom and legs bare as she helped her parents mend their nets in a coastal village outside the capital through which Christina had often ridden on her Saturday morning gallop; the lovely young German she had caught kissing one of her clerks when she suddenly turned the corner outside the Council Chamber; a woman prostitute who stood challengingly outside the porch door of the Great Church, laughing at the clergy who refused her admission and boldly eyeing the married men entering with their wives for Sunday service. . . .

And all these figures, as Christina strove in her dreams to approach and talk to them, were transformed at the last second into Ebba.

In the weeks and months of intimate friendship which followed, Christina's adoration of Ebba developed rapidly.

Neither of the girls saw anything basically wrong in their association, nor did any of the courtiers at first suspect that the close friendship was yet another stage on the way towards the disaster which was to befall their Queen and country.

Masculine homosexuality existed among the mercenaries of the army, particularly among the German ex-prisoners, but it was so rare that no army regulation on discipline referred to it.

After the fashion of invading armies, it was expected and accepted that conquered towns would supply women for the troops and there were in any event the usual train of baggage carriers, itinerant merchants and harlots battening on the fighting men.

Women's emotional and sexual outlook was not even considered, and the majority would have laughed to scorn the idea that women could love spontaneously and without the tinder of a man's touch.

Consequently no one was concerned as to what was happening in the Royal apartments.

Because Christina was by this time accepted as being plain to the point of ugliness even those nearest to her did not realize that the uninteresting husk of her outward appearance hid a highly emotional and romantic nature.

From her mother she had inherited a temperament in which the virtues and vices of the emotions were given full rein; by her father she had been endowed with the sexual strength which had made him a heroic lover when in his youth he sowed his wild oats.

He was also the man who above all others had sought to teach his daughter to glory in physical strength.

Christina had been deprived of the loosely knit association of playmates and affectionate adults during the years of childhood when such friendships are the principal guard against youthful distress and loneliness.

Now in puberty she was impelled by a redoubled force not to miss the emotional alliance and yearning for expression which is the second stage of a young woman's development.

She yearned for beauty in the grey world of her Northern palace and amidst the ascetic and serious men who surrounded her. She longed for love – to receive and give the proof of its existence.

Ebba Sparre, vain and pretty, sulky and vivacious by turns, was as softly feminine as Christina was the antithesis of a gentle girl.

Ebba felt neither revulsion nor delight when Christina's greeting became a cloying embrace.

She did not appear to dislike the Queen's habit of stroking her soft hair and caressing her hands when they talked together.

Nor did she challenge Christina's ridiculous excuses of feeling cold or being afraid of the dark which brought her hurrying into her bed – making their proximity an excuse for the blissful tenderness of an embrace that for the first time in Christina's life gave her a sense of security and purpose.

Ebba's only reaction, if she bothered her silly head about the matter at all, was that she seemed to have found herself a new admirer.

The effect on Christina was more profound.

While the homosexual phase was as temporary as it is with most girls who indulge in a deep and jealous friendship with another girl or endure agonies of doubts and hopes with a 'crush' on an older woman, the mental attitude lasted long after the physical and emotional aberration had passed.

The absurdity of transvestism had been thrust on her long before she herself adopted it.

From the moment the Royal astrologers had implanted the belief in her mother's mind that the child-to-be was a prince, Christina's masculine outlook began.

It was nourished with care by her father, his officers, and the guardians who followed them.

Only her Aunt Catharine had tried to guide her gently into feminine ways, attempting to teach her embroidery, pretty manners, and the wholly feminine art of doing nothing charmingly.

Despite Christina's love for her aunt, the attempt failed utterly. By the time she was ten the guilt complex about her unmistakably feminine body was so strong that her dexterity,

64

so apt when it came to marksmanship, fencing, or writing, fumbled with the embroidery needle until the piece was thrown aside in a passion.

Everything seemed to conspire to her masculinity. She was a King in name; she did a man's work in a man's world.

As men could hold their heads high despite the pitted marks of the pox, the ugly scar of the sabre slash, or the bloated obesity of lascivious living, so she could ignore her crippled shoulder, her large feet, and swarthy complexion.

Her appearance became more mannish; she startled even a tolerant Court by the soldiers' oaths she used on the most incongruous occasions.

The servants came to know the heavy tread of her feet as she stumped around the palace in men's shoes, which were a size too large for her.

She achieved her ambition. The contrast between herself and the soft and feminine Ebba became as marked to the onlooker as that between a lover and his sweetheart. Christina was well content.

The hurt of her mother's perfidy to Sweden and the insult of the rejection of her proffered reconciliation were both erased by the receptive pleasure of Ebba as Christina tried in a hundred pathetic ways to show her adoration.

The intensity of her love began to give her warning to keep the liaison personal and private, if only because her regard appeared absurd.

When she was twelve years old Christina had gone to the quay to say farewell to the first Swedish settlers in the New World.

Like most literate children she had devoured the accounts of the explorers who travelled in the wake of Columbus and the sight of these men and women setting out for a new life in a country on the other side of the world moved her greatly.

Oxenstierna was completely bewildered by the young Queen's constant request for news.

When a message eventually arrived that the Swedish colonists had settled on the banks of the Delaware River, Christina was overjoyed, and for once refused to study the dispatches from the war fronts.

News after that was sporadic but early in 1642 came a report that more arrivals justified a little township and that in honour of the Queen the place was to be called Fort Christina.

The Queen tried to arouse Ebba's enthusiasm in the settlers, but when the young Countess learned that there was no evidence of the gold and silver in the Delaware basin comparable with the riches available to the Spaniards farther south she pouted with boredom.

Christina did not blame her companion for a moment. She felt that the failure was entirely hers.

She must have lacked the imagination to describe the wonder of such a constructive effort in an age of destruction; she was overselfish in her pride of the fort named after her.

'There will be more Swedish villages soon, and forts to protect them against the red savages,' she said suddenly. 'I shall order them to name the next one Fort Ebba – or perhaps Fort Belle, for by reports the country is as beautiful as you, my dearest friend.'

Ebba smiled vaguely, conscious that there must be some honour in the idea, although she could not see the personal advantages.

But morning brought common sense and caution.

The sight of solemn-faced Oxenstierna banished the proposal on Christina's lips. She confined herself to writing a brief message of approval and good wishes to the governor of Fort Christina.

From that morning her relationship with Ebba became more secretive. By nature Christina was frank and honest-minded. Prudence and deceit had no place in her make-up. For that reason the unfamiliar trait became the more intriguing and enticing.

No Swedish courtier saw anything but a sickly giggling friendship in the inseparable companionship of Christina and Ebba, but there was one man, by place of birth a subject of the Vasas, but by ancestry and outlook wholly French, who watched with amusement.

Count Magnus de la Gardie had special privileges in the palaces of Stockholm and Uppsala, for his mother was the entrancing Ebba Brahe, up to the time of her marriage the mistress of Gustavus Adolphus.

At the time of her wedding it was whispered that the nuptial knot was tied at the direct behest of the King and that considerable moneys and land were handed over, not as a gift to an old friend and an old flame, but for the purpose of concealment of the expected fruits of the Royal liaison.

Suffice it to say that Magnus's father, Jacob, had come to

Sweden comparatively unknown and yet had after his marriage emerged as one of the most wealthy and influential of all the immigrants. He became a field-marshal and supreme head of the Court.

Magnus, said to be the most handsome man in all Europe, had been educated in France.

He was as lazy as a man blessed with a brilliant brain can be, preferring to skim the generalities of culture instead of turning himself into a pedant by the study that was available to him and of which he was perfectly capable.

He returned to Sweden, but little disturbed by the recurring crises of the war and equipped with a tolerant contempt for the rugged and uncouth behaviour of those around him.

Most of all he was amused by the perverted romance of the Queen.

It did not shock him at all. He had read the works of Grecian and Roman writers on homosexuality and had followed the conventional practice of young students in Paris of experimentation in perversion.

He bided his time with patience, the patience born of the cynicism of satiety at an age when he should have still believed in the magic of love.

'I believe the Queen will be weary of her love of this girl,' he told his valet – the only man in his confidence. 'When that happens she will doubtless be hungry for the other amusements of Eros.'

'My master would be an excellent tutor,' the servant murmured. 'It will be my duty to keep my ears open. There is a maid of the Queen's bedchamber, a buxom young woman, who eyes me with some favour. I shall make it my business to seduce her, and thereby obtain a reliable informant.'

'Truly the lowborn share the delights of us all,' sighed Magnus, 'and sometimes even their intelligence. You have ever been a good servant. When your information is useful you will not be unrewarded.'

'Of course,' said the valet thoughtfully, emboldened by this praise, 'there are perhaps obstacles to the fulfilment of the desires that my master's charm and finesse will doubtless arouse in the Queen's breast . . .'

He stopped, not daring to voice his thoughts more frankly.

Magnus de la Gardie was perfectly aware of what the man meant. In his student days when the glory and reputation of

67

Gustavus Adolphus had come up in political discussion, he had never been loath to insinuate that the Royal blood of the Vasas flowed in his own veins.

He did not really believe it, for he had inherited the outlook and many physical characteristics of his legal father, but there was always the lingering and absorbing doubt.

Yet that the possibility of Royal paternity would mean that any liaison with Christina would be incestuous worried him not at all.

De la Gardie's opportunity came more quickly than he had expected. Ebba Sparre's feelings were quite impersonal about the devotion of her mistress – so impersonal that she flirted with any likely man she came across.

Usually she had the sense to be reasonably discreet about it, and none of her love affairs became more than sporadic incidents, with the objects of her coquetry constantly changing.

But when one of the secretaries with a foreign embassy, who neither knew nor cared about the jealous possessiveness of the Queen, pursued his attentions so well that Ebba met him late one night, the storm broke.

As the dishevelled and flushed Ebba crept to her room long after midnight she found Christina standing by her dressing-table, shaking with suppressed fury. There was nothing of the hurt and pleading lover about her.

'You are depraved, wanton, a harlot,' she raved and lashed at Ebba, with a tongue dipped in acid.

She frightened her with threats that as a Queen she was perfectly capable of sending her to prison for conspiracy.

Ebba, terrified for once out of her stupid complacency, burst into tears and Christina's anger passed. She fell on her knees begging forgiveness and then kissed and caressed Ebba wildly and passionately, pleading for her love and her constancy.

Ebba swore her devotion and reiterated over and over again that she forgave Christina for her harsh words.

She did not know why the Queen should feel so deeply about a male rival, but she had the animal sense to feel frightened. The threats had not been empty ones.

The two girls believed in their reconciliation, and their love affair with one another was now resumed, but an invisible but very tangible barrier had arisen between them. Christina had emerged from an emotional fever.

It left her once more lonely and unwanted.

Count Magnus saw the signs of her disquiet and prepared the setting in which their romance could flourish with consummate care. He was not in the least impressed that a Queen should look on him with favour, but he did see that with such a mistress he could obtain considerable wealth.

He was not greedy for power, for he was too lazy, and as regards influence his very name automatically provided him with privileges and political facilities more than sufficient to enable him to enjoy his inconsequential design for living. But, like all hedonists, he was constantly in financial difficulties.

His father, who was perfectly ready to provide him with a magnificent house, a fine coach, and a retinue of servants, was unsympathetic to repeated demands for money to settle gambling debts and to quieten the parents of the various young women he had seduced.

Christina became so enamoured of the handsome young Count that she saw nothing absurd in his moaning about money when it would have been more natural for him to speak of love.

He would lie at his ease in one of the beautifully furnished salons of the la Gardie palace while Christina stroked his forehead with her strong but sensitive fingers.

As if in a reverie he would recount his worries and voice his hope that her fingers would banish the wearisome drumming in his brain. Christina fell easily into the trap.

While delighting in the suggestion that her caressing fingers could achieve the miracle she made it more certain by making him lavish gifts of money, gold ornaments, and even privileges of the Crown.

From such small beginnings as a gold chain and a bag of coins to settle a tailor's bill the stream of gifts to the insatiable Magnus reached a fantastic total.

Christina neither knew nor cared how much money he obtained on her permission from the Royal coffers and she had no qualms about paying for the enormous number of precious objects which she bought him from the dealers who besieged the Palace.

But the Government knew of her gifts of land, for the conveyances had to be registered by notaries.

Before her eyes were opened to the Count's cold and calculating attitude she had presented him with estates producing a revenue of the incredible sum of 80,000 rix dollars a year.

This income was a loss to the State, for the lands were the source of national revenue while they remained Crown property. Once they were transferred to Magnus he was not liable even for taxation on them.

In return for this lavish generosity Christina obtained a little temporary happiness although she received no flattery and no adoration.

Magnus was not particularly enamoured of the inexperienced girl whose only romantic experiments had been of a callow nature with little more than fondling and girlish caresses as the evidence of her yearnings.

Moreover, she was ugly of face and gawky of body and he regarded himself as a connoisseur of women as of everything else.

As much as he dared he made his relationship with Christina one of theoretical love-making.

He talked to her of his own erotic adventures and he coloured their discussions on art and literature with a sexual flavour which aroused Christina's desires and accentuated her hunger for love in whatever form it was presented to her.

When they were together in public the Queen would hang on Magnus's arm like a lovesick girl.

In private their discretion was so great that it bred gossip of a more damaging character than would have been the case if they had ostentatiously lived together.

Those who understood the real character of the young Count suspected that he was a sadist. Even if they did not know the word, they knew of the cruel perversions which serve it.

If the truth could be revealed it would probably show that Magnus was as bored with sex as Christina was bewitched by it.

Like so many men who attained satiety too early in life he only found pleasure in the degradation of love.

He had the vicious intelligence to realize that fundamentally the Queen dreaded the day when her heart should rule her brain, and he pandered to this by confirming her worst suspicions that sexual love lowered human beings to a bestial level rather than raised them to Divine heights.

If Christina inwardly recoiled in horror from the entertainments the Court arranged for her in the la Gardie Palace, lonely and discreetly distant from the capital, she managed to hide it.

She was acutely envious of his worldly knowledge and laughed uproariously to disguise her innocence and trembling revulsion.

Coarseness had always amused her, but Magnus's concept of humour was something quite alien to her.

Gradually she forced herself to talk brightly about it, and sometimes to provide a little amusement in return. She had neither the finesse nor the degraded mind of Magnus and the result was crude comedy rather than dangerous eroticism.

One of her ideas pleased her so much that she extended it to the Palace and amused guests with it for years afterwards.

She obtained a book of indecent songs and taught a bevy of girls to sing them parrot fashion. The choir was trained by experienced teachers and sang beautifully.

The unfortunate girls, little more than children, had no idea whatever of the obscenities they were mouthing.

Some time during the fervour of her adoration of Magnus it was said that Christina gave herself to him. Members of the Senate were delighted when they heard the rumour, for it seemed to banish their fears that the Queen would never lie in the arms of a man.

If she could yield to Magnus she would surely marry, and the problem of the succession would then be solved.

That intimacy took place between Magnus and Christina is not to be doubted. Its form remains a mystery. Magnus, wary lest he should fall out of favour if he boasted of his dominance over the Queen, refused to talk even during his drinking bouts with his cronies.

He was aware that Charles Gustavus had a special place in Christina's heart, and he suspected that her many reminiscences of their childhood affections were told so as to divert his mind from the rumours that since then they had on occasion become lovers.

If the rumours were true, and the point is very debatable, it could have been only a fleeting infatuation on Christina's part because Charles Gustavus, small, dark and stocky, slow-brained and taciturn, was not Christina's ideal in any way.

As a child Christina had laughed at his unquestioning obedience to discipline, and she was openly contemptuous of his pomposity as he grew older.

There is, however, little doubt that she did for a short while think romantically about him, if only because he was for a time the only male companion she saw frequently, and also because her deeply passionate nature urged her to experiment in sex.

From Magnus's point of view, however, Charles was undoubtedly a formidable rival. He could not risk throwing the Queen back into her cousin's arms simply in retaliation for his own lack of discretion.

Later, when Christina regretted the tawdry events that had taken place between Magnus and herself and they had become enemies, she was told that he had once revealed what had occurred between them.

'You have published a secret which I resolved to have concealed all my lifetime,' she wrote to him. 'In making this known you show yourself unworthy of the good fortune you derived from my friendship.'

If Magnus did tell all, Christina took immediate steps to silence those who knew their secret.

No one ever passed on that tit-bit of gossip – not even in later years when scandal about the outrageous Queen swept in a thousand true and untrue stories across the face of Europe.

CHAPTER SIX

On Christina's eighteenth birthday, the Estates met in Stockholm in order to conduct the formal handing over of the nation to the Queen, and to hear an account of the work of the Regency.

Christina, who by this time had a valet instead of a tiring maid, was persuaded to dress with unusual care.

She was escorted to the great hall by a long procession of officers and statesmen. The silver throne had been moved to the dais, and was covered with a purple canopy.

She was asked to take the oath as King of Sweden, promising to maintain the national religion, the ceremonies of the Court, and to observe the form of Government approved by her father.

She took the oath in a clear and emotionless voice, showing sincerity if little excitement.

Then, one by one, the Regents gave a report on their administration of affairs since the death of Gustavus Adolphus, principally complaining of the great economic difficulties with which they had wrestled.

As soon as their more depressing reports had been given and heard in silence, the representative of the nobles rose and asked that the Queen should confirm their numerous privileges, not the least of which was complete exemption from taxation.

Rather shortly the Queen assented, but to the consternation of Oxenstierna and many of the old guard, she refused to discuss the details of Government, telling the Estates:

'Our many pressing embarrassments mean that we have not had the leisure to examine the matter accurately and it is our wish that we postpone full consideration of this subject until after our Coronation.'

It was noted that Christina was speaking in the Royal plural.

This was a form of address which hitherto she had usually ignored, despite the repeated suggestions of her tutors and the Regency that, as Queen, she had few privileges to speak personally and must always voice her thoughts as those of the whole Swedish nation.

Afterwards she met privately a group of the leading statesmen who promptly questioned her on the question of marriage.

They told her that many of the Ambassadors in Stockholm were discreetly approaching the Government with suggestions about various eligible men, both young and old, who could give Sweden a marriage of great political advantage.

When Christina's darkening face told them that this was dangerous and futile talk she was asked outright about her regard for Charles Gustavus.

He had loved her in a quiet restrained manner which was characteristic of him, but Christina had forced their relationship into more emotional and dramatic channels.

To her chagrin she learned that a letter she had sent him earlier in the year was known to the Government. It ran:

'Beloved Kinsman,—I see by your letters that you do not dare to commit your thoughts to the pen. Yet we can write to one another with all freedom, if you will send me the key to a cipher, and compose your letters according to it, and put the initials C.R. on the address as well as inside, sealing it at the same time with a different seal expressly devised for that purpose as I do with mine. The letters can then be sent to your sister, the Princess Maria.

'We must observe every possible precaution for people have never been so much against us as now. But they shall effect nothing, if only you will remain as firm as I hope. People talk a great deal about the Elector, but neither he nor anyone else in the world, rich as he may be, shall ever turn me from you.

'My love is so strong that it can only be overcome by death; and if, which God forbid, you should die before me, my heart shall be dead for every other, but its memory and affection shall follow you to eternity, and there abide with you.

'It may be that someone will advise you to demand my hand now and openly, but I implore you by all that is sacred to have patience for yet a year, till you have won more experience in war, and I myself have got the crown on my head. I beg you not to let yourself think the time too long, but to remember the old saying,

"He waits not too long who waits for something good."
'I hope, with God's help, that it may be a good we both wait for.'

When the sentiments she had expressed were repeated to her, she tossed her head angrily and said that in the meantime her regard for Charles had lessened considerably.

'If you are able to delve into my private affairs as you seemingly have done in the case of this note written by a mere girl on the spur of the moment,' she said, 'you will know that my correspondence since that time has told the Prince that my affection is that of a friend, and not of a love-struck girl.'

Oxenstierna glowered at her and said:

'Your Majesty will doubtless remember the well-known proverb which states that human beings are not born for their own sakes but for the sake of their country; this I dare suggest applies even more strongly in the case of a virgin Queen.'

The air in the Chamber was tense.

Everyone present knew that underlying the impersonal suggestion of the Chancellor there was his intimate family interest in Christina's marriage.

He had not been the most powerful man in Sweden, with even more political influence on civic affairs than Gustavus Adolphus himself, for the whole of his adult life, without taking to his character a certain belief that he could aim at a Royal lineage for his descendants.

He doted on his son John and, spurred by his ambition and by his qualms about the young Queen's capriciousness, he had for some years envisaged marriage between Christina and John Oxenstierna.

John was good-looking and not without the heritage of brilliance his family always showed. But the constant inculcation during his childhood of the belief in his high destiny had made him pompous and intolerant.

In his meetings with Christina he made the smallest possible gesture of obeisance, and he did not hesitate to show his disapproval of her views when they did not precisely coincide with those of his father.

On occasion their conversation on Swedish war policy degenerated into bickering, with Christina terminating the argument by ordering him out of her presence.

Axel Oxenstierna, desiring to prepare his son for high office arranged for him to be the Swedish plenipotentiary at the peace conference at Osnabruck. Christina insisted on a second delegate and chose Adler Salvius.

The son of an obscure tradesman, Salvius had risen rapidly in his political career after he had impressed Gustavus Adolphus with his ability as a civil governor.

The Queen chose well. Salvius was a rarity in his world and age – a man of peace.

That he managed to maintain and enhance his prestige in a government where anything but a bellicose attitude was almost akin to treachery said much for his persuasive and convincing tongue.

'He has the capacity to work all men to the desired end,' Christina said when Oxenstierna began to grumble about the appointment.

She forestalled the contemptuous allusion she guessed was coming about the lowly birth of Salvius by adding: 'There are peasants who are chosen to act as princes, just as there are princes who behave like peasants.'

Oxenstierna had perforce to acquiesce to Salvius's appointment.

Although the Regency could have countermanded Christina's order, he knew that his son was really quite unfit for the delicate negotiations which lay ahead.

Vain and insular in thought, John Oxenstierna was able to do little but deny every proposal of the allies in the belief that obstinacy would in time defeat the calculating French, who were anxious that Sweden should not be left the most powerful nation beyond the Rhine.

Salvius, on the other hand, was always ready to give way on little points in order to achieve a larger one.

His mind was as flexible as Christina's, and in the interminable negotiations which went on for years Salvius was the voice of Sweden and John Oxenstierna the sullen and constantly outwitted false echo.

The dispute between the Queen and Chancellor over the peace delegation was heightened by the rumours which had reached Christina's ears.

She learned with anger from Count Magnus and her valet that John had been persuaded to expect a Royal marriage as his Queen's reward for success at Osnabruck.

Apart from Christina's natural resentment at this usurpation of her personal wishes John Oxenstierna represented everything in a husband she looked on with distaste.

Cold, didactic and unsentimental, he presented an ascetic attitude to the world while it was known that his amorous amusements were both crude and ephemeral. He essayed the pompous eminence of his father without the reputation or talent to justify it.

Christina hated him – and she began to hate the father who could even think that she could consider marriage with such a man.

This situation was known to everyone at the Council meeting, and most of the statesmen there became uneasy at the thought of the inevitable scene when personalities would be hurled by Queen and Chancellor.

Fortunately Christina evaded the trouble by stalking out of the room.

As soon as she reached her own apartment she sent for Magnus and told him of the pressing demands of the State Council on the marriage question.

'I realize,' she confessed, 'that most of them are thinking only of Sweden.'

Magnus laughed away her worries, telling her that as Queen she had no need to bother about such suggestions from those who were bound by oath to obey her.

At this time Christina had made another intimate friendship with a man whose entire background was coloured by the French attitude that she so greatly admired since she had come under the dominance of Magnus.

This was Pierre Chanut, a charming attractive man of forty-four whose main interest was the arts and who dabbled in politics as a hobby. He had been sent to Stockholm as the personal representative of Anne of Austria.

Christina took to him on the day that he came to the Palace to present his credentials, and Chanut became the first platonic friend she had made.

He did in fact become her unofficial tutor, guiding her tastes for reading and discussing with her books and paintings with all the regard of one expert for another.

The Queen was deeply flattered by his approval of her opinions and in the early months of 1645 when Christina made various Royal progresses about the country, Chanut was invited to accompany her, sitting beside her in the coach while Ebba Sparre was allowed to daydream on the seat opposite.

It was on these long and uncomfortable journeys through a country where roads were virtually unknown, and which were an almost impossible morass in the spring thaw, that the talk turned gradually to more intimate thoughts.

The Queen found that Chanut neither approved nor disapproved of her affairs with Ebba and Magnus, but he showed that he could understand her loathing of the idea of servitude in marriage.

There is no doubt that the French diplomat was tremendously impressed with the young Queen. With amazing discretion he omitted any unpleasant details about her when he made his reports to his superiors.

'Her authority arises from her personal good qualities. A King of like virtue would be absolute in his Senate; in any case that would be less surprising than to see a girl turning as she will the minds of so many old and wise councillors.

'It is no wonder that she displays the prudence of a man in the Senate, seeing that in action Nature has refused her none of those qualities of which a young cavalier would brag. She sleeps little and usually stays in bed only five hours though she is sometimes obliged to sleep an hour after dinner.

'Nothing is important in her eyes except the ambition of making herself renowned for extraordinary merit rather than conquest. She loves to owe her reputation to herself, rather than to the worth of her subjects.'

Christina's regard for Chanut slowly banished her infatuation for Magnus, and probably at the diplomat's suggestion, she arranged for him to marry one of the most eligible and beautiful young women in the country, Marie Euphrosyne, daughter of the Palsgrave.

At the same time she persuaded Magnus' brother, a colourless young man named Jacob, to marry Ebba Sparre.

In this way she ostensibly got rid of two emotional entanglements which Chanut impressed on her would damage her character if she continued them.

'The fact that these marriages will silence the criticism which is being noised abroad,' he suggested, 'will not prevent you from continuing the liaisons in secret.'

In truth Christina had become tired of Magnus just at the time when he had found himself falling in love with her. His innate cynicism prevented him from making any fuss and he agreed to the marriage with Marie Euphrosyne, particularly when Christina promised to make him Captain of the Guards and to bestow on him a large pension.

The Queen, knowing that she could retain his affection should she ever feel any need of it, flattered him still more by appointing him in 1646 as Ambassador to France.

She lavished money on her ex-lover and the Embassy which set out for France cost the nation 100,000 rix dollars.

Three of the finest warships in the Swedish Navy escorted the packet with Magnus (without his bride) and his staff to the French coast.

Chanut had written to his friends in Paris to explain that the new Ambassador was an intimate friend of the Queen, and that the possibility of his eventual marriage to her could not be ruled out despite the arranged union with Marie.

As a result, Count Magnus was treated with inordinate honour when he arrived, and Magnus did little to deny the rumours that he might one day be Prince Consort of Sweden.

Little did he know that in Stockholm Christina had already almost forgotten him.

She had launched into a campaign of turning her capital into the cultural centre of Europe, believing, despite Chanut's gentle protests, that all she needed to do was to buy any object of art on which she could lay her hands.

Her representatives travelled far and wide in Europe buying up complete libraries in Italy, searching in Greece for classical statues, ranging through the great châteaux of France to purchase pictures.

This mass of material arrived at the Palace in Stockholm to add to the congestion of the loot obtained from Central Europe by the Swedish armies.

Room after room was crammed with books. They stood in piles in the passages while alterations were made to turn yet another room into a library.

The complete lack of knowledge on how such fragile things should be stored meant that many of them were ruined in the damp and draughty passages.

It could be at least said for the Queen that she saw her collecting mania through to the end.

She was up the moment it was light, and pored over her dusty treasures long before they had been put in order. She realized that her genuine love of knowledge was being ill-directed by her own immature tastes, and, at the suggestion of Chanut, she wrote for advice to Descartes, the most famous philosopher of his day.

It was typical of her that, as an excuse to pave the way to invite him to be her guest for an indeterminate period, she sent him a philosophical question –

'When one makes a bad use of love or hate, which of these abuses is the worse?'

Descartes, who had a magnificent brain but very little heart, did his best to answer the question though he knew nothing whatever about love.

Perhaps, however, he had heard enough about his Royal correspondent's character to give her the answer she wanted.

'When pushed to a vicious extreme,' he answered, 'love is the more dangerous.'

In her consuming ambition to make Sweden the modern Greece, the centre of the sciences and arts, Christina forgot that Athens had been famed in its age as a martial nation, spreading her commerce behind the standards which went to war against every country that bordered her own.

If she had realized this she might have seen that the historical parallel was closer than she could ever make it.

Sweden had burst by soldierly vigour through the confines of older and richer nations. In the slowness of time she would mature as a nation of culture, science and commerce.

That development lay three hundred years ahead, a dream of which Christina neither knew nor cared.

Searching for balm for her tormented mind, hating the physical desires which burned in her body, and longing to have a mind which was complete mistress of her emotions, she had long revelled in the stories of Descartes's intellectual power.

Perhaps only a handful of people in any century seriously ask themselves 'what is truth?'

In the seventeenth century there were certainly two: the meditative René Descartes and the neurotic Christina. The older of the two had got nearer to the answer and the younger envied him for it.

'All that we know,' Christina heard he had proclaimed in a

world that believed it knew everything, 'is as nothing compared with that which remains to be known.'

She felt the spiritual longing of a lonely, wisdom-hungry soul when she read –

'My aim is to attain certainty, to clear away loose earth and sand until I reach rock or clay. We get nearer perfection when we know instead of doubting.'

Doubts were the bugbear of Christina's life – doubts about her destiny as a Queen, doubts about the religion she had sworn to uphold, doubts about the hedonistic cynicism of Magnus, doubts about the adorable perfection of Ebba . . . doubts girdled her in chains.

To break their links the Queen's librarian was ordered to pen the letter of invitation to the insignificant, untidy little man who lived like a hermit in the Netherlands.

He took a long time to obey the behest which was in effect a Royal command, while the finest Swedish vessel available impatiently awaited his pleasure in a Dutch harbour.

In October, 1649, he set out for Stockholm, incongruously decked out in courtier's dress instead of his usual black monkish habit.

Christina had prepared a lavish feast to mark his arrival. He sat through the meal in a reverie, ignoring the meat and wine, answering his companion's attempts at conversation absentmindedly or not at all. Christina was impressed. She thought him a demi-god.

Everyone else, with the exception of Chanut who already knew Descartes well, thought the philosopher a crank – and a dangerous crank at that.

For a little over three months all Christina's amorous amusements, and all but the most pressing affairs of State, were forgotten while she talked hour after hour with Descartes.

The old man, who was a devout Catholic, was both bewildered and dominated by her personality.

He felt that he could not disobey the Royal commands, and even when the bitter weather of a Swedish winter gave him a cold which turned to pneumonia, he still obeyed Christina and duly arrived every morning at five o'clock to talk philosophy in her library, where the only heat came from a tiled fireplace with the remains of the previous day's logs.

Her insensitiveness to his illness destroyed him.

Descartes was found dead in bed on the morning of February

1, 1650. Christina was both heart-broken and conscience-stricken.

She summoned the City Council and told them that she intended to give him a Royal funeral. The Council dissuaded her with difficulty, but she managed to ensure that the ceremony at his burial became both ostentatious and expensive.

When she returned to the Palace she shut herself in and would see nobody for the rest of the day.

Once again she was alone. Magnus was enjoying himself in Paris, and Ebba Sparre was perfectly happy with her husband in one of the La Gardie Palaces.

In the spring of 1650, Axel Oxenstierna fell ill, and his absence from the State Council gave Christina the opportunity she needed to take over more autocratic powers.

It was typical of her quixotic nature that she simultaneously made plans for an expensive and ostentatious Coronation, and, at the same time, busied herself with the possibility of abdication.

Later she claimed that her desire to leave the throne was due entirely to her religious beliefs, and in her usual manner of talking to her God as one person to another, she confessed to Him –

'The Swedish Chancellor was one of the greatest obstacles I have had to overcome in order to carry out my design of sacrificing all to Thee.'

Oxenstierna's illness temporarily removed this obstacle, and in March, 1650, she sent the Secretary to the Court to the old man's bedroom in his house on the outskirts of Stockholm with an Act of Succession which he was supposed to sign without argument.

The Chancellor would not even read it.

'Will you tell Her Majesty,' he said, 'that I have little knowledge of this matter, and I cannot have it claimed that I ever had a hand in it. I assume that the Senate have contrived this document at the behest of the Queen. If they had taken my opinion on it I could have given them better advice and I would have prevented the haste in which it has been drawn up.'

The old man sat up in bed, and quivered with anger.

'You can assure the Queen that if at this moment I saw my grave open before me, and I had to choose either to get in or sign this Act, the Devil fly off with me if I would not rather die than sign this instrument.'

He quietened a little and added softly, almost to himself:

'My consolation lies chiefly in my old age, which will prevent me from seeing the sad times that are to come. Others may say that I am an old fool, understanding nothing of these affairs, but I will not sign.'

'But the rest of the Senators and the Estates have all consented, Your Excellency,' protested the Secretary.

'Are their hearts all writing tablets,' the Chancellor demanded, 'that Her Majesty is able to read them like a book? If she could really do this, she would see written there quite other things – how few of my colleagues are sincere in this matter.'

He sighed and began to read the document.

'I will stand out no longer now that things have gone so far,' he admitted at last, 'but I wish here and now to stand excused before God and my country, for I am convinced that this affair will end badly for Sweden.'

When the Secretary returned to the Palace and began to report to the impatient Christina the gist of this conversation she refused to listen, saying that all that mattered to her was that he had signed the Act.

Nevertheless she let the Senate know of her displeasure at Oxenstierna's antagonism. But she had won the day. Charles Gustavus was named the heir to the throne in the event of her dying without issue.

She forced through her wish that he should be titled Prince of Sweden and given an annual income of 50,000 thalers.

But because she wished to keep entirely in her own hands the precise time when he should take over the Kingdom from her, she forestalled all suggestions from the worried Senate that he should hold some office under the Crown.

Charles was present at this Council meeting. He was a patient man and probably knew better than any of the Councillors how things were going.

For this reason he willingly acquiesced to Christina's orders that he should do nothing to divide the allegiance of the country.

He took a solemn oath to recognize the Queen as his monarch, and to make no move whatever without her advice and approval.

With this triumph in her hand, Christina devoted her attention to the plans for her Coronation.

She loved spectacle, and without consultation with the Estates she made many lavish arrangements which could not really be afforded.

Although the country was anxious that her sovereignty should be confirmed now that she was of age, so involved and majestic were her plans that it proved impossible for it to take place until October 30, 1650.

Prior to this the date had been announced by the Government and almost immediately postponed by the Queen time after time.

In justice to her it must be admitted that she was anxious that the Divine blessing of her throne should not occur while any vestige of the Thirty Years War remained to cloud it.

In this she was completely sincere.

She did not intend that her Coronation should be anything but a magnificent celebration of the beginning of an era of peace.

The usual place for the crowning of the Kings of Sweden was Uppsala, but Christina threw away tradition and insisted that it should be held in Stockholm.

One reason was that even she realized the prohibitive expense of conveying everything and everybody to the tiny little University town, and another was that she realized far more people would see her if she went in procession through the streets of Stockholm.

A fortnight before the ceremony she unaccountably left the Palace and went to live in the mansion of Jacob de la Gardie.

Her excuse was that she wished to withdraw from the sight of her people and then make a formal entry into her capital.

Whatever her real motive may have been, La Gardie was highly flattered by her presence and began to spend enormous sums of money to entertain her.

He promised, for instance, that in the grounds of his mansion there would be four fountains which would spout wine for days on end.

Despite Christina's sudden decision to leave the capital she soon found that she could not bear to be away from the scene of activity and three days after she left she announced that she intended to return.

Her orders were that she would look with favour on all persons who made her journey of a little over four miles between the La Gardie mansion and the Palace a notably ceremonious one.

This message had the desired effect and shortly after midday the Nobles and Estates began to arrive in their hundreds.

At two o'clock Christina considered that there were sufficient people to make a procession, and she set out in her coach.

At the head of the procession was a regiment of cavalry. They were followed by five companies of the Royal Guards. Then came the carriages of the Senators, the Nobles, and the Foreign Ambassadors.

Although Christina hated the feminine flavour of her Court, she agreed that her Ladies-in-Waiting should take part in the procession, and they followed the Ambassadors.

Behind them came the mounted State Trumpeters, and immediately preceding the Queen's coach was the carriage conveying Charles Gustavus.

Christina herself rode in a carriage which was covered entirely with black velvet embroidered in gold. Around it marched a company of archers and her footmen.

As the procession approached the town, Christina was delighted to see that the Senators had erected a triumphal arch.

This seemed all the more miraculous to her because there had been no sign of it when she had passed along that road three days earlier.

It was, in fact, a gimcrack piece of work built of wood and covered with canvas, painted so that it looked like stone. Around it were various hurriedly painted pictures of Sweden's victories during the war and emblems portraying the might of the Vasas.

Above the arch fluttered scores of battle standards and pennants which had been captured during the Thirty Years War.

In the centre was a long inscription praising Christina for all the good work she had done since she became Queen.

Christina ordered her coachmen to drive more slowly so that she could receive the adulation of the people. Having done this, she then leaned back so that they were unable to see her.

The moment she reached the castle she summoned the Commander-in-Chief of her army and ordered all the cannon to begin firing salutes until she gave the order to stop. The command was duly obeyed and went on for two hours.

Everywhere in the town, on the islands around the city, and in the Swedish battleships anchored along the coast, the noise boomed out until nearly 1,000 salutes had been given.

That night a banquet was given in the Palace, at which the meal itself lasted for three hours. Christina sat through it all, hardly eating anything.

The next two days she employed in receiving hundreds of officials of the Government of the town and of the clergy, to check up on the minutest details of the actual ceremony, and to receive gifts from every state and township in the country.

The Coronation took place on a Sunday, and the procession to the Great Church was even longer and more splendid than that which had brought her to the city. The actual service was taken by the Archbishop.

After he had preached the sermon, Oxenstierna stepped forward and read out the oath of the Kings of Sweden with more than necessary firmness and slowness.

Christina repeated in a loud voice and met the challenging glance of the Chancellor without blinking.

She was then anointed and the Crown of Sweden placed on her head.

The Officers of State approached one by one and presented to her the Sword, the Sceptre, the Golden Apple and the Keys of the Kingdom. The Queen stood during this part of the ceremony, and then a herald came forward and shouted:

'The most powerful Queen Christina is crowned, her self and none other.'

She moved to her throne against the High Altar with the Chiefs of the Army and Prince Charles at her side.

For more than an hour she sat stock-still while the members of the Government came forward, knelt and took the Oath of Fidelity. The service had taken nearly three hours.

On leaving the church, Christina entered an open triumphal carriage specially built for the purpose and covered with gilt. It was drawn by four milk-white horses.

One of the Court Treasurers walked ahead of her carriage throwing gold and silver souvenirs to the townspeople. As soon as she arrived at the Palace she again ordered the cannon to fire a salute.

Although it had been arranged that she should rest for some hours, Christina rejected the pleas of her ladies-in-waiting and spent the rest of the afternoon standing on the battlements listening to the roar of cannon.

That evening another banquet was held and as all the guests were given accommodation in the Palace it continued on and off for three days, simply because the tireless and excited Christina never made any formal dismissal of her guests.

Not unexpectedly, the Wednesday was an anti-climax when everybody slept from sheer exhaustion.

After this respite the Queen resumed the celebrations, for she still had a number of novelties with which to entertain her guests.

At a tournament which she impatiently watched, she cut short the feats of horsemanship and knightly valour by ordering a young officer of the Palace Guard with whom she was particularly friendly to bring on a special novelty that they had devised together.

It was a triumphal cart festooned with devices glorifying Christina which rumbled across the arena without any visible means of motion.

Later that day her guests went with her to an open space where a miniature mountain had been built, as usual of wood and canvas, on which the most beautiful women she could find in Sweden lolled in the guises of Muses while a small orchestra hidden inside the faked mountain played music.

The various officials of Stockholm were not to be outdone by the Queen's own ingenuities in celebrating her Coronation.

All over the town entertainments were provided to which she went with the greatest enthusiasm.

One set-piece was made to represent the superiority of women over men, and another was a pyramid on which women portrayed three Queens of the Amazons while at the peak a vacant place suggested to everybody that a Queen superior to the other three had now been crowned.

At the end of the week the Chancellor and some members of the City Council attempted to persuade Christina to spare a morning for serious conversation about the Government of the country.

She blithely told them that for the moment she had absolutely no time for this.

'My Nobles insist on giving one banquet after another in my honour,' she told them, 'and it would be impolite of me to ignore their invitations.'

Oxenstierna withdrew in helpless anger.

Neither he nor the members of his party attended the latter revels, but the Queen enjoyed every moment of them, and seemed to be oblivious of the sullen, glowering looks which surrounded her as she moved about the city.

The common people had been thrilled and excited by the actual Coronation, but the reckless waste of money as the celebrations went on and on made them think of the cost and of their own poverty and privations.

There were murmurs of resentment and rebellion which did not go unnoticed by those who disliked and distrusted Christina.

CHAPTER SEVEN

THE death of Descartes left Christina without a guide and friend, and for a time she resumed her intimacy with Count Magnus, whom she ordered back from France.

Then, early in 1651, she learned that her mother had decided to return to Sweden.

Maria Eleanora had found that she was no happier in the country of her birth than she had been in Denmark. Her arrival was made in state, and Christina once again tried to effect a reconciliation by going personally to greet her when she landed at Nyköping.

The interview between mother and daughter was stormy and inevitably it had a profound effect on Christina's nerves.

What was said while the two women sat together in the Queen Mother's private apartments is not known, but afterwards, while Christina was having supper, she suddenly collapsed and remained unconscious for an hour.

The next day she was taken back to Stockholm, where the Court doctors started their cures, their only knowledge being of old-fashioned herbal remedies chosen according to the astrological horoscope of the patient plus the comparatively novel method of blood-letting.

The Queen regained her health quite quickly in spite of the treatment. Typical of her doctors' attitude was the serious advice of one of them, who said:

'These attacks of yours are due to your sober living. You drink too much water and insufficient wine. You waste your strength by preferring fruit to meat.'

Despite Christina's brusque dismissal of any queries about her health from her friends, she was in fact very worried about herself. And she was glad when Salmatius, one of the learned men that she had attracted to her, insisted that she should obtain better advice.

This philosopher had been living in the private apartments of the Queen for some months, despite constant messages from his employers, the University of Leyden, who demanded his return.

Salmatius was a bad-tempered man who was hated by the Swedish statesmen and courtiers, even more than most of Christina's intellectual idols.

He quarrelled with almost everybody, but the Queen was so enamoured of his learning that even when he was rude to her, she did not complain.

He warned her that she was rapidly becoming an invalid – a fact which perturbed him because a constant stream of presents and his hopes of a large pension seemed in jeopardy.

'Unfortunately in all Sweden there are no learned doctors,' Christina replied. 'It is characteristic of my country to be as ignorant of medical matters as of any other form of science.'

'I can assure Your Majesty that it would be easy for you to engage one of the best doctors in the world,' Salmatius answered. 'He is a friend of mine named the Abbé Bourdelot.'

Salmatius had chosen his opportunity wisely.

Instantly Christina demanded full details of the Abbé and by that afternoon a courier was on his way to France ordering Bourdelot to attend the Queen.

This doctor was a charlatan but not more so than any fashionable practitioner of his day.

He had been a boyhood friend of Salmatius in the little town of Sens where Bourdelot's father, a man named Michon, ran an apothecary's shop. Bourdelot's uncle had been a well-known Parisian doctor and his nephew inherited his medical books and equipment on his death.

His name and reputation young Michon simply adopted for himself.

The new Bourdelot launched himself on a career which quickly made him a fortune.

Although he had for a time been physician to the Pope, he did not ignore the wonderful opportunity of enhancing his reputation as doctor to a Queen.

Within two months he arrived in Stockholm, and, to the consternation of the Court, he forbade any of the doctors then attending Christina to see her again.

Christina was delighted with this, but she was not so pleased when he also ordered that none of the professors should see her either.

Strangely enough, she did not countermand this order as she

would have done with practically anybody else, for it seemed that she had instantly fallen under the mesmeric spell of Bourdelot, which was his principal asset as a physician.

He was not, however, without common sense even though his medical training was virtually non-existent.

He realized from all the stories that pervaded Europe that the Queen, with her three hours' sleep a night, her reading at four o'clock in the morning, and her revelries until past midnight, had taxed her strength to the limit.

He ordered her to take what, in fact, was a rest cure, and, to the amazement of the Palace kitchens, he demanded the most curious items of food.

Milk and boiled water were the only drinks he allowed, while the very fruits which the Queen's doctors had stated to be the source of her trouble became the principal feature of her diet.

On his orders, the Queen sent messengers to France, Italy and Spain to bring her grapes, melons and oranges. By the time they arrived, little of the fruit was eatable, and the cost of providing even a light midday meal became prohibitive.

But the regimen succeeded, and Christina rapidly recovered her energy even if her nerves remained on edge.

Having proved to her that he had almost magical knowledge of the weaknesses of the mind and body, Bourdelot began to create a more intimate friendship that further alarmed the Swedish people.

During Christina's convalescence Bourdelot became her constant companion.

One of the strange features of his treatment, which had intrigued women in both France and Italy, was to sing to his patients while accompanying himself on a guitar. He rarely sat at the bedside without providing this sort of entertainment.

It was not quite so ridiculous as it appeared to other people, for almost all his patients were neurotic, and he chose gentle and soothing melodies which eased their nerves and indeed often sent them to sleep.

He also believed that perfumes had a strong effect on the mind and body and he brought a large variety of them to Stockholm.

Some of these were aphrodisiacs and their effect intrigued Christina so much that she suggested to Bourdelot that they should experiment together in discovering more.

A small laboratory was set up in one of the Palace rooms, and here the Queen and her doctor would spend hours playing about with extracts of flowers and much more noisome fluids in an attempt to create a new and potent fragrance.

They tested their experiments on themselves, and as, of course, few of them worked, the comical atmosphere appealed to both of them.

Statesmen in the courtyard of the Palace would shake their heads in consternation as peals of laughter emerged from the room to which entry was absolutely forbidden.

It also concealed other secrets, and the rumours that the Queen and Bourdelot were dabbling in black magic were not without foundation.

The Frenchman had among his uncle's books a number of weird treatises and methods of summoning the powers of evil, and to these Christina could contribute some of her own knowledge of the witchcraft which still flourished in the Northern part of her country.

She also engaged language experts to translate various strange Arabic manuscripts that she had bought some time previously merely as valuable curiosities.

The work captivated both the doctor and the Queen, and it was an interest that neither of them ever lost. Later in her life Christina spent a fortune on trying to make gold and to discover the elixir of life.

Their work together put the Queen completely under the dominance of Bourdelot and he vaunted his power in every possible way.

He realized that his greatest enemies were the learned men who still remained in Christina's employment, even if she no longer had much conversation with them.

His methods of getting rid of them were effective even if they were cruel, but they had the result of creating still more enemies.

There were two old men who were genuinely interested in Swedish folklore.

Christina had offered them accommodation and an income so that they could pursue their studies in peace and quiet. One of them was interested in music and the other in the dances of the country.

Bourdelot constantly told the Queen how useless and pointless their research was, and when she replied that the work was not without interest and value, he arranged to expose their pretensions.

He told the researchers that on the Queen's order they were to give a practical demonstration of their work. One was to dance and the other was to sing. As they were both well over sixty and their knowledge was purely theoretical, the result was both painful and ludicrous.

Some of those who were in the audience were so disgusted that they walked out, but Christina was helpless with laughter.

Then the old man who had been trying to sing stopped suddenly, walked over to Bourdelot and hit him across the face. The Queen promptly stopped laughing and later banished him from the country.

On another occasion a clergyman was to read his paper on the geography of the Holy Land. Bourdelot was alarmed to hear that the work was a remarkable one, and that the Queen had shown special interest in it.

To prevent her attending he suddenly insisted that she must be bled, and then rest in her room. To make certain he gave her a narcotic and she slept for ten hours.

The lecturer was not told of the circumstances and so both he and the sycophants of the Court believed that he had in some way gained Christina's displeasure.

When she woke up and learned that the lecture had taken place, she was angry, but such was the powerful personality of Bourdelot that without question she accepted his statement that had she attended she would have risked her life.

There was no limit to the ambition of Bourdelot to gain absolute mastery over the Queen.

He even managed to turn her completely against Count Magnus, and in some cases it seems probable that he caused the death of senators whom he regarded as powerful enough to be dangerous.

In any event, two or three of them unaccountably died when he treated them for minor ailments.

The scandal of Christina's intimacy with the doctor spread from Stockholm to all the capitals of Europe, and it was heightened when a third person joined the inseparable couple. What his duties were remained a mystery, although many bizarre stories were told about him.

There was a man-servant from France, he was unbelievably

good-looking and inordinately proud of his hair which was as long as a woman's.

At Bourdelot's suggestion the young man, whose name was Poisonnet, was ordered by Christina to dress as a girl, and she insisted on him wearing girl's clothes wherever he went.

The ordinary people of Stockholm did not perhaps care deeply about the private activities which went on in the Palace, but they were disgusted with Christina's behaviour when she attended Church service.

As usual, Bourdelot and Poisonnet, dressed as a woman, sat on either side of her. Sometimes she would ostentatiously read a book during the sermon, and if she did not read she yawned and shifted restlessly on her chair.

Once she brought her dogs with her and romped with them during the actual service.

At other times Bourdelot would talk with her in a loud voice, making amusing comments on the preacher and on members of the congregation, and Christina would roar with laughter.

The doctor had made no secret of the fact that he was an atheist and there were many there who believed with horror that the Queen, who had taken an oath to defend the tenets of her faith, was also beginning to deny the existence of God.

Only a few people, and one of them was Bourdelot, knew that all this disgraceful behaviour deliberately carried on in front of her people and before her bishops, was not proof of her disbelief, but alarming evidence of her change of belief.

She had perhaps a heavy sense of guilt at her way of life. She was beginning to realize that she was a scandalous monarch.

She had long realized that she had hopelessly failed the vaunting faith of her father in her destiny; and she knew that her thoughts, and a growing number of her actions, were steeped in wickedness.

As always, in her mind all was well just beyond the horizon if only she could reach it.

In the few brief hours of nocturnal rest when she was alone and lonely, Christina felt a gnawing hunger for Divine help for the future, and for absolution from the past.

These emotions were perhaps passing ones, but they were strong enough in their impact during the weakening hours of one day's death and another's birth to remain vividly in her brain.

Superstitious and always groping for a sign, she believed that it came one morning when she was due to confer with Don Joseph Pinto Pereira, the Portuguese Ambassador.

He was a rather dull old man who spoke no languages other than his own, and his secretary acted as interpreter. When Pereira entered the audience chamber the Queen was surprised to see a Jesuit priest accompanying him. Quickly the Ambassador apologized.

'My secretary is sick, Your Majesty,' he explained in Portuguese. 'I trust that you will permit my confessor, Father Macedo, to interpret for us.'

Macedo translated the words and the Queen replied that she had no objection. The business of the morning continued, when to the Jesuit's utter amazement Christina suddenly said:

'I wish to consult someone of your creed and Order. It is a matter of the greatest secrecy.'

Macedo turned to the Ambassador.

'The Queen wishes to know something of our nation's explorations,' he lied, while he fought to conceal his emotions.

Old Pereira beamed. This unpredictable young woman had never shown any interest in his country's history. He launched into his favourite subject.

The exploits of Vasco da Gama occupied the next hour but Christina heard nothing of them. The priest, with brilliant cunning, passed on to the Ambassador her alleged comments, while he answered her torrent of questions about the Catholic religion.

Not once on that morning, or during many other audiences when the long tales of Portuguese voyages were recounted, did the Ambassador suspect what was afoot.

Macedo fully realized the importance of Christina's hints.

The tolerance to Catholic priests living in the privileged territory of the diplomats' palaces in Stockholm was meticulously observed by the Swedish authorities, but the precise letter of the law and no more was obeyed.

Macedo was accustomed to insults when he moved through the streets. He knew that he was in the capital of the bitterest foe of Rome and he knew that the woman who showed such avid desire for knowledge of his faith was the figurehead of all the powers of heresy ranged against his Church.

In those strange bilingual meetings the priest poured out his soul and Christina glowed with a new joy. Here, though she did not say so, was the balm she needed.

When the Jesuit judged he could do no more he annoyed his master by demanding permission to return to Portugal because the cold of the North was undermining his health. Pereira would not let him go, whereupon Macedo asked the Queen to facilitate his journey.

Within three weeks he was telling his almost unbelievable story in Rome. There had already been rumours about Christina's beliefs, but rumours meant nothing.

The insignificant confessor's story, born of fact, bore the stamp of truth. In the uttermost secrecy, for a false step might unleash the dogs of war, Rome prepared a plan.

Secretive as the deliberations on the wisest move may have been in Rome, the Queen was not quite so discreet. She bubbled over with excitement and let drop hints that something of great personal importance was afoot.

Oxenstierna and his party heard none of them, for by this time their contacts with the throne were almost entirely official and formal. But Magnus, back from France, was greatly perturbed.

He did not care personally if the Queen reverted to the primitive worship of Odin and Thor. Indeed, he would have preferred this because it would have at least been an atavistic action that the Swedish people could understand.

But the brittle conversation she made on the spectacular attractions of Catholicism was, as he well knew, something neither the country's leaders nor the common people would endure.

He saw his dreams of an easy life of secret power and unlimited wealth evaporating every day.

He knew that even the exotic amusements he offered for her entertainment had begun to bore her so that she often failed to attend them. Things had always come easily to him.

Now that he faced unfamiliar failure he exhibited venom and started ruthless intrigue.

He staked everything on his belief that Christina loved him more than she loved Bourdelot, and he formally protested that the French doctor had slandered his character in gossip with some courtiers.

He expected the Queen to rush to his defence. He was wrong. She left Bourdelot to fight his own battles, which he did with such consummate brilliance that it was the Count who lost.

Christina had some time earlier appointed her first lover to be Grand Treasurer, an office he filled to the personal benefit of both the Queen and himself.

He knew that the Royal finances were in such a muddle that it would be difficult, if not impossible, for the Queen to dismiss him and appoint someone less clever but more honest.

Accordingly he played what he believed to be his trump card.

Wearing the hurt look of a misunderstood lover he craved permission to retire to his country house. Christina instantly refused, saying that his presence in Stockholm was necessary for business reasons.

Utterly miserable, Count Magnus endured the situation of being merely an official who had to send a request in writing before he could gain audience. Then he began his intrigues again and sought to dispose of his rivals by more instances of slander.

Christina called his bluff on each occasion, and when he again requested to have permission to retire she snapped:

'We not only permit it, but order you to do so.'

Count Magnus hung around the Palace for two days.

The Queen did not relent and as a last resort he wrote a frantic letter pledging his love and loyalty. He persuaded the Queen's courier, Prince Adolphus, to take this to Christina in person.

She read it over and dropped it on the floor.

'Poor Count!' was all she said.

Every means in his power was used by Magnus to regain his position. He bribed and persuaded powerful interests in the Senate to intercede on his behalf.

He even approached Oxenstierna, who mildly quoted the words the Count had used to describe the Chancellor when he held him in nothing but contempt.

'You once said that I am in my dotage, already in my second childhood, and am no longer capable of giving advice,' he observed. 'Obviously I cannot help you.'

While Magnus brooded on revenge in a castle a hundred miles from Stockholm, Bourdelot's star continued to shine brilliantly. But the time came when he, too, found that the intimate meetings became shorter and rarer.

He accepted the situation philosophically.

His ambitions were smaller than those of Count Magnus, and he had amassed a considerable fortune during his brief stay in Stockholm. Wisely he packed his bags and took his leave before he was dismissed.

On arrival in Paris he wrote the Queen a friendly note. When it arrived Christina looked at the florid writing on the cover, held it to her nose and exclaimed,

'It smells of physic.'

Then she threw it among the logs of the fire without reading it.

Magnus and Bourdelot were already extinguished flames of past loves. There was a more warming and illuminating emotional fire to occupy her attention.

Christina, as Queen of Sweden, was bored with her responsibilities. She was one of those restless souls who long for something and, having attained it, find the fulfilled ambition banal and empty.

A Queen in the sight of God and her subjects, she discovered that the exalted position brought little but more loneliness.

It did not lessen the enervating routine of daily State work nor open up familiar paths for her to tread. And being tired of her lovers, life was becoming unendurable.

For some time she had devoted her attention to entertainments and amusements to titillate her emotions. Dances, revels and masquerades became an almost nightly occurrence.

As they were held on Sundays as well as weekdays an increasing number of Swedish aristocrats, after listening to the attacks in the Sunday morning sermons on such infringements of Holy Writ, excused themselves from being in attendance.

Christina had a passion for fancy dress, which gave her an excuse to appear as a boy or, by contrast, in the exotic dress of a Moorish concubine.

Such disguises also pleased her because she could order them to be French, or classical Greek, or Castilian.

The sight of the banqueting hall cleared of anyone who faintly resembled a contemporary Swedish subject delighted her and for a few hours at least she could believed that she had transformed her kingdom from the ascetic atmosphere of Scandinavia to a land of culture, sun, and romantic dalliance.

Often these entertainments would degenerate into practical joking and horse-play which had little connection with the theme she had ordered for the occasion, and at these times Christina would be the life of the party.

She loved dancing, but she used so much energy that it became more of a physical exercise than an art. She put all the spirit she could into her performance, whirling round long after her partners were breathless.

As she was the only person present who did not indulge in the lavish quantities of refreshment available she was often giving a solo performance while the rest of the company was comatose.

Even Christina could not help but notice that fewer and fewer courtiers were accepting her invitations, despite the presents of jewels and ornaments which were little more than bribes to her guests.

Perturbed at this loss of popularity, she decided to increase the prestige of those who were still favourable to her ideas by forming a secret society.

She pondered over the plan for some time.

The original inspiration came from Count Magnus who had earlier intrigued her with details of exclusive groups in Paris who safeguarded themselves against scandal and rumour by instituting an order with its members taking an oath of secrecy of what went on at their meetings.

Christina was thrilled and intrigued by the idea but she had little notion of the purpose of such societies, and even the frank conversations of Magnus did not really enlighten her.

But a secret society she would have. She announced its formation at a 'Banquet of the Gods' at which she appeared as a Greek shepherdess and Magnus was an extremely handsome Apollo.

A few political adventurers and foreign exiles were present, dressed as Greek gods.

There was also a darkly handsome man in the costume of Mars. He was Don Antonio Pimentelli, the Spanish Ambassador.

His brief in Sweden was to arrange a treaty between the two countries and also to sound the real political attitude of the Queen to France.

He was a man who held women in contempt, simply because his handsome face and supercilious manner seemed instantly to make them his devoted slaves.

He boasted that he found their conquest so easy that it was repellent to his desires. Nevertheless, he believed that Christina might be interesting.

He had heard that she was unusually temperamental. He expected that for once there might be some savour in a minor battle before the inevitable conquest.

Flattery was the weapon he always used with women, showing his admiration so blatantly that he was amazed that any woman could regard it in any manner except that of insult.

When he came to the Palace to present his credentials he walked through the door of the audience chamber, and stepped forward resolutely to where Christina was lolling in a chair.

Then his steps began to falter and at some distance from her he paused, stared, and bowed, keeping his eyes fixed on her.

He backed away without a word and passed through the doors, but not before he had seen that Christina had laid down her book and was staring after him in amazement.

The next morning he sent an aide-de-camp to crave a further audience.

This time Christina was sitting majestically upright in ceremonial robes, and there were guards who shut the doors as soon as he was in the room.

Pimentelli bowed and after handing over his credentials began a rambling eulogy of the honour he felt in having the post at the Swedish Court.

Christina listened in silence as long as she could, but soon she angrily demanded why he had behaved in such a peculiar manner on the previous day.

Pimentelli made a helpless gesture.

'It was unforgivable, Your Majesty,' he confessed. 'But I was so much struck with Your Majesty's presence that it was essential that I should have time in which to collect myself.'

He looked at her with his dark, half-closed eyes, his body taut with suppressed devotion. Christina simpered like a peasant girl and was lost for words.

If she had known him better she would have seen the light in his eyes disappear and his body relax. In a trice he was the formal ambassador. This Queen, after all, was no different from other women.

She was the typical willing and, therefore, uninteresting victim of his charm.

He disguised the truth of his contempt for her because his diplomatic duties demanded it. Even when the Queen insisted that he move into a suite at the Palace so that they could meet in intimacy whenever she wished, he kept the comedy going.

The love-making she demanded was provided with as much efficiency as a report on Spanish exports and imports – and with as much real emotion.

He soon discovered her liking for bawdy stories and he arranged for his staff to tell him a few jokes before he left for his *tête-à-tête* in the Queen's apartments each evening.

Christina loved his poker face as he recited the obscenities of the Stockholm quayside and drinking dens. She did not realize that to him the stories were insupportably pointless and crude.

Pimentelli made the best of circumstance. He was able to increase his own wealth and influence as the doyen of the diplomats in Stockholm.

Foreign traders who wanted concessions, diplomats of countries friendly to Spain who required an interview the Queen would otherwise have had no inclination to grant, all found it advantageous to have Pimentelli pave the way for them.

Even Swedish statesmen who could not proceed with the nation's business because they lacked the Royal seal sought his help.

Some would frankly admit their envy of his position of influence and of the intimacies which it permitted. Pimentelli, discreet in all other things, could not let the insinuation pass.

He would damn the Queen's womanly attractions by stressing her intellectual abilities.

'She is of an admirable spirit and courage beyond her sex,' he once told Whitelocke, the English ambassador. 'She is well skilled in military affairs, and as fit as a woman possibly could be to lead an army.'

It was not the sort of eulogy that any infatuated woman, not even the ebullient Christina, would have relished from her lover.

Such was the man who stood in the costume of Mars beside the rather ridiculous-looking Shepherdess. It was seen that on

Christina's revealing dress a gold brooch was pinned at the breast. It consisted of a double A, the two letters inverted.

That evening there was little revelling. Christina spent the whole time explaining the purpose of the Order of Amaranta. What the aims were is now unknown. Christina and the eventual thirty members – fifteen men and fifteen women – obeyed the oath to keep the society secret.

It did become known, however, that the unmarried members had to swear never to marry, while the married members promised never to remarry when their spouses died. Ebba Sparre was in the Order and Christina was already regretting the marriage she had arranged for her girlhood sweetheart.

All that the courtiers and State officials who were not asked to join could learn about Aramanta horrified them.

They knew that the badges Christina had ordered were not the simple gold emblem she had worn at the revel. They were encrusted with diamonds and beautifully worked.

They also knew that Antonio Pimentelli came from the town of Aramantha, and the coincidence of the two A's of his Christian name and birthplace was a disturbing one.

They equally disliked the motto engraved on the badge: 'Memory is sweet.'

Not even the members of Aramanta were permitted to the innermost confidences of their leader. Only Pimentelli heard the truth.

In the quiet hours after passion was satiated Christina one night told him that her life was nearing a critical climax.

'You will perhaps be in Stockholm for many years,' she whispered. 'I shall be far away, but there will be one unbreakable link between us. We shall be of the same religion.'

Pimentelli made no answer. He was calculating on the possible advantages to Spain that could emerge from this sensational upheaval. And he wondered if it was the exaggerated talk of a restless woman or the irrefutable decision of a Queen.

Even he had not been told of the strange visitors who had furtively visited the Palace a few days before.

CHAPTER EIGHT

It was late in the evening of a March day in 1652 that two men, cloaked and wearing large black hats, disembarked from a small merchant ship which had put in to Stockholm.

They wandered round the streets looking for an inn where they could stay the night.

Rosenhane, a Senator, had been talking with one of Christina's equerries, and as they left a drinking-house on their way to their homes, they saw the two strangers standing in the street.

At such a time it was unusual to see men who were not obviously Swedish abroad so late in the day, and immediately suspicious, they asked them their business.

The first man, Francesco Malines, groped for words in German, and explained that he and his friend were gentlemen of leisure from Italy, uninterested in politics, but fascinated by the many stories they had heard of Sweden's greatness.

He explained that they had been travelling through Europe and now hoped to see both the beauty of the Scandinavian country and the glory of her culture.

Immediately the suspicions of Rosenhane and the equerry were dissipated, and they escorted the travellers to the best inn in Stockholm and ordered the innkeeper to do everything to make his guests at home.

The equerry, whose name was Wachtmeister, on his return to the Palace, met Christina who had just completed her simple evening meal and was walking restlessly through the dark and chilly rooms of her home.

As was usual, she demanded to know what he had been doing, the motive being both the suspicion of everyone who was not in love with her and her jealousy that her servants had more freedom to do as they pleased than she had.

The equerry mentioned that he had been talking to the Senator and added in a flattering tone:

'One thing would have pleased Your Majesty. As we left

the inn we fell in with two Italian gentlemen. They appeared to be quite poor from the appearance of their dress, but in fact, from their conversation, they are undoubtedly men of wealth and culture. Such is the fame of Your Majesty's contribution to learning that it appears they have travelled all this way to pay homage to Sweden's greatness.'

He did not notice Christina start or note her sudden eagerness of manner. Nor did he see anything strange in her suppressed excitement when she dismissed him. As he bowed from her presence she asked:

'What was the name of the inn at which these strangers are staying?'

'We took them to the "Golden Cock" which we considered would be the most comfortable, Your Majesty,' he replied.

As soon as he had gone, Christina went to her own apartments and wrote a brief note.

She called a young peasant boy whom she had engaged as a personal page because he was too stupid to know the import of any orders she gave and too devoted to her to break any trust she put in him.

'I want you to go as quickly as you can to the "Golden Cock",' she said, 'and deliver this note to two gentlemen from Italy who are staying there. If you go immediately they will no doubt be having their evening meal, and it will not be necessary for you to approach the landlord first. Come straight back and tell me their answer.'

The boy nodded as he muttered to himself his orders. Within half an hour he had returned and was alone with Christina.

'The gentlemen were very pleased with the message, Your Majesty. They asked me to bring them here at once.'

'You did not bring them to the main doors of the Palace?' she demanded angrily.

The boy looked mystified.

'No,' he answered. 'They told me they would prefer to wait in the alley which runs past the servants' quarters until Your Majesty gave them permission to enter.'

Christina nodded.

'That is well,' she answered. 'Now go and bring them to me. It would be best for them to go through the kitchens, and see that no one molests them on the way.'

The servants were too well disciplined by their hot-tempered mistress to question the appearance of two cloaked figures led by the boy who they knew was the guide for many of her lovers and cronies.

Perhaps their only surprise was that on this occasion there were two men, not one, and they smirked with amusement at the idea of still another strange carousal which would continue far into the night.

But they were wrong. When Christina had heard of two visitors from Italy, she had correctly guessed the reason for their journey.

The elder of the two, Malines, was in fact Professor of Theology at Turin, and one of the leading authorities on the Catholic religion in Europe. His friend, Paolo Cassati, was a Professor of Mathematics in Rome, and a personal friend of the Pope.

When they entered the room where Christina eagerly awaited them, she dismissed the page-boy and could hardly wait to whisper, as if the very walls of her private boudoir had ears:

'Have you any letters for me?'

It was Cassati who answered.

'Yes, Your Majesty,' he replied, 'but we did not bring them with us fearing possibly that this invitation was a trick. They are safely hidden at the inn.'

'That is well,' Christina replied. 'Do not mention them to anyone. Doubtless there will be people who will guess why you are here, but without the letters they cannot be certain.'

They talked for some time – mostly of religion. Then as suddenly as Christina had ordered them to her presence, she dismissed them.

In the succeeding days the two Italian gentlemen were constantly at the Palace, ostensibly giving the Queen advice on the binding of her books, the latest trends in Western European architecture, and on the hanging of her paintings.

The interviews were, of course, concerned entirely with spiritual matters. The two men had come to see if she was a fit person to be received into the Catholic Church, and their orders from the Pope were to question her closely on her religious views.

In fact it was they who were questioned.

The Queen indulged in the most abstruse questions of

philosophy – the immortality of the soul, and the real distinction between the different sects of Christianity.

Malines was as much surprised by her knowledge of the subject as he was disturbed by the many doubts that she showed as regards the eternal truth of Rome.

Cassati felt that all the optimistic views he had been given at the Vatican about the readiness of this strange woman to make a gesture which would rock the forces opposing Catholicism throughout the world, had been very much exaggerated.

But there came the day when the unpredictable Christina abandoned all her arguments and said with an almost hysterical giggle:

'You would not think I was very close to becoming a Catholic, would you?'

The men did not answer, being amazed at this abrupt change on a morning when she had been particularly critical about everything they told her. Eventually Cassati murmured:

'Your words make us feel like men raised from the dead, Your Majesty.'

Christina instantly found new objections.

'I suppose the Pope would permit me to take Communion by the Lutheran rites?' she demanded. 'Say once a year – to please my people?'

Cassati shook his head.

'It would be utterly impossible,' he answered.

Christina walked across to the window and looked out at the great bulk of the parish church of Stockholm where she had so often worshipped in company with her people.

Without turning round, and so quietly that her guests hardly heard her, she said:

'Then there is no help for it. I must give up my throne.'

The men stole from the room, knowing that their mission had ended in triumph. They remained at the inn a few days more, hoping for a further summons. None came.

Instead Christina sent the little page-boy with some letters. They included one to the Pope and another to Cardinal Chigi.

In them there was little about her own views on conversion. They were filled with queries as to the house that would be provided for her if she came to live in Rome; questions regarding the expenses that she would have to meet as a Queen without a throne, and many demands that she should be treated with all the regard due to royalty.

With these letters the two visitors departed from Stockholm as quietly as they had come. On the same day that their ship cast off from the quayside, another vessel was putting out to sea.

In it was a Royal courier carrying a long and rambling letter from Christina to Prince Frederick of Hesse, trying to persuade him of the wickedness of taking the step of changing his religion, precisely as she herself was doing. Her message ended:

'You see, I keep my word and avoid burying myself in religious matters. We are born with the sceptre and arms. After making our profession so loud, it would be profane to enter religious controversy. We of Royal blood must take care not to play the theologian.'

Whatever the suspicions of the greatest in the land may have been, whatever rumours rippled through the Courts of Europe, it is certain that none outside her most intimate circle knew how inevitable it was that Christina would abdicate.

For months she awaited impatiently for the turn of fate which she believed would provide the opportunity she wanted. When it did not come, she took matters into her own hands and sent a letter to Charles Gustavus ordering him to come and see her. They met in her private study, and without looking up from the papers with which she was dealing, she said:

'You had better start interesting yourself in State affairs, for it will not be long before you will have to deal with them. I have now definitely made up my mind to abdicate.'

Her cousin started and said irritably:

'I cannot believe that you really intend to take this step! Frankly, Christina, I have become so accustomed to your emotional outbursts that I very rarely believe what you say!'

Christina looked at him with surprise and anger. Even though she despised the man she had once loved, she was still anxious to be regarded highly by him.

Few people dared to tell her what she knew to be the truth, that she was emotionally unstable and prone to making proposals which she had no intention of carrying out.

'You may not believe me at the moment,' she replied, 'but in a few days I shall certainly be able to convince you. You will see down at the quayside at Goteborg the crates in which I am sending out of the country all my books and manuscripts and my personal possessions.'

Charles Gustavus laughed.

'If you are doing that,' he said, 'you may be able to abdicate, but you certainly will not be able to leave Sweden. The people of Goteborg will realize what those crates mean and the Government will forbid you to leave the country.'

'You are wrong,' Christina retorted. 'I have already told many people in the Palace that I intend to take a long holiday in Pomerania and they have accepted such an idea as reasonable. They believe that I am going there so that I can think about the problem of the succession without being worried by the day-to-day affairs of State.'

Charles shrugged his shoulders. Even though he had not received permission to leave, he walked to the door, and without bowing, left her to herself.

It was the first time that this quiet and decorous Prince had ever shown anything but a slavish loyalty to Christina. And not for many years did he reveal that he had been the first of her Swedish subjects to know that she definitely intended to leave the throne.

Nearly a year passed before she told Oxenstierna that she wished him to call a full meeting of the Diet at which she proposed to make an important announcement.

The old Chancellor, suspecting what that announcement would be, told her that before he could summon the Diet, the nature of the announcement would have to be discussed with the Senate.

This meeting was arranged for a day or two later, and at it Christina brusquely informed them that she proposed to announce her resignation as Queen, and to obtain the formal permission of the Diet.

The Members of the Senate were dumbfounded that she did not ask their advice even as to the form her announcement should take. A few of them begged her to alter her mind.

The meeting degenerated into an argument which Christina settled by striding out of the room. When, at their request, she agreed to meet them again a week later, she simply repeated her implacable resolve.

The aged Count Brahe was one who showed no sorrow or pity. He stood up, his face red and mottled with anger.

'The Queen is deserting her post, and that is something a Vasa has never done!' he cried. 'I cannot believe that she would have even thought of this step unless it be that some of those with whom she is infatuated have given her this dastardly advice.'

The Queen met his challenge.

'You are going too far, sir,' she told him, and added with a cynical smile, 'You know as well as I do that there are many in this country who will hear of my abdication with great pleasure. Do not ask me the real reason for my decision, for you will realize it soon enough.'

The Count endeavoured to protest further, but the domineering eye of the Queen effectively silenced him.

Oxenstierna, the man who had met the challenge of the greatest and most ruthless men of Europe with unflinching mental courage, simply gave way to tears and made no attempt to change her decision.

All he could do was to whisper, 'The Diet shall hear you.'

His shock and grief merely annoyed Christina. She showed no sign of conscience or of sympathy for the destruction of all that for which her Chancellor had worked ceaselessly and with unflinching loyalty.

When she had gone the members sat in complete silence, then Oxenstierna moved to a desk and began writing.

The quill moved slowly across the parchment and the others did not speak while he completed his task, guessing that in his words would be the feelings of them all.

When he had finished and signed his name, he handed the parchment to Brahe and told him to read it aloud. The old man, in quivering tones, began . . .

'We do not know that Your Majesty would lead a more peaceful life after abdicating, for we cannot see into the future. Nor are we convinced that a private life would be consistent with Your Majesty's duties. Cares and anxieties are common to all men. Especially do they fall upon Sovereigns whose duty it is to seek their pleasure and to find happiness in work.'

All the members added their names below Oxenstierna's and a servant was told to take the memorandum to the Queen immediately.

She read through it quickly, and then with a gesture of defiance threw it on the floor.

'Tell the Senate,' she ordered the servant, 'that the message I will soon send them is the day when they will summon the Estates to hear my decision.'

Christina delayed the meeting until 11 May. In the meantime she forced both Charles Gustavus and Oxenstierna to discuss with her the various details of her abdication.

She was intensely greedy and demanded fantastic revenues from the country she had already impoverished. Only on this point – and simply because it was impossible to meet them – did the two men refuse her requests.

On the matter of the succession they gave way in every detail.

When in a moment of generosity she tried to placate her one-time friends and advisers by stating that she intended to make Oxenstierna and Brahe dukes, the old Chancellor shook his head.

'There are already too many dukes in Sweden, created by your hand, Madam,' he said coldly. 'The country cannot afford the honour, neither do we desire it.'

The meeting of the Diet was held in Uppsala, the ancient city of Sweden's Kings and Government.

Christina drove there a few days before, through villages which were sullen and silent at her passing. When she left the castle on the first day of her arrival to walk around the ancient city there were men and women in the streets who spat as she passed by.

A few children dared to throw stones and were cuffed by the guards who followed her. Christina's only reaction was to smile.

She climbed to the great heathen temple which lay on a hill above the old city. Telling the guards to let her go alone on the last part of her pilgrimage, she reached the summit by herself.

Below her the countryside lay beautiful in the sunshine, while around her the ruins recalled the long story of Sweden's glory which she was leaving behind her for a purpose she still hardly understood.

After three hours of meditation she returned to the sombre half-built castle.

Until the Diet meeting Christina was left alone both by her friends and Ministers. On the morning of 11 May, she rose early.

When she was ready the Master of Ceremonies came to her apartments to escort her to the Great Hall where the Senate had assembled. He left her in an ante-chamber where the guards stood at attention.

After she had been offered and refused refreshment, the doors were opened and she walked through the rows of benches covered with red cloth to a dais at the far end.

Here stood the Chair of State made of silver and shielded by a canopy of crimson velvet. On each side were crimson stools for the chief statesmen of her realm.

There were some murmurs as the Queen passed through the hundreds of people assembled there because her head was uncovered.

It was an insult to the ceremonial which provided that everyone in the room except the reigning monarch should have caps to doff to the covered Sovereign.

Some of the Members of the Diet showed their indignation by keeping their hats on, but all stood to show their deference to the throne.

When the Queen reached the throne she sat down, and for several minutes there was complete silence. Christina was nonplussed, for she knew that it was Oxenstierna's duty to inaugurate the Diet by an introductory speech.

Imperiously she beckoned him over and demanded that he should outline the business of the day. He told her quite truly that he was unable to mouth the words.

Hardly knowing what to do, Christina dismissed the Chancellor and again there was a silence marred only by the disturbances in the body of the hall.

Eventually Christina took the matter into her own hands, and standing up, she said:

'I think that the Diet is aware of the reason for this meeting. I have long ago made up my mind to abdicate. I believe that it will be for the good of my country, and nothing can alter my resolution.

'I thank you for your loyalty, and I hope that you will remember me as having always wished to serve our most dear country as best I can.

'I have nothing more to say except to hope that all my work be to the glory of God, to the advancement of the Christian Church, and to the good and prosperity of our country and all her inhabitants.'

The brief speech was heard in absolute silence and again there was a hiatus in the procedure while Christina sat on the throne and the Members of the Diet stared at her.

The aged Archbishop of Uppsala was the first to move. He

walked from his stool and, standing in the passageway between the benches, bowed deeply to the Queen.

Then the old man began an oration on which he had been working for many days.

It was a rambling and fulsome eulogy which bore little relation to the facts, and the Queen showed her boredom by shifting restlessly and looking from side to side while he spoke.

When the Archbishop had finished and advanced to kiss her hand, she barely thrust it forward, and refused to look at him.

Various other speeches followed, all of them of the same kind, and all ending with an entreaty to desist from her intention. She treated them all in the same way as she had the speech of the Archbishop.

Finally a peasant member at the back of the hall could endure the farce no longer. He elbowed his way to the front and voiced the opinion of the majority of the Members when he said:

'Lord God, Madam, what do you mean to do? It troubles us to hear you speak of forsaking those who love you so well as we do. Can you be better than you are? You are Queen of all these countries, and if you leave this large Kingdom, where will you get such another? If you should do it, as I hope you won't for all this, both you and we shall have cause, when it is too late, to be sorry for it.

'Therefore my fellows and I pray you to think better on't, and to keep your crown on your head. Then you will keep your honour and our peace; but if you lay it down in my conscience you will endanger all. Continue in your gears, good Madam, and be the fore-horse as long as you live, and we will help you the best we can to bear your burden.

'Your father was an honest gentleman and a good king, and very stirring in the world. We obeyed him and loved him as long as he lived. You are his own child and have governed us well, and we love you with all our hearts.

'And the Prince is an honest gentleman and when the time comes we shall be ready to do our duties to him as we do to you. But as long as you live we are not willing to part with you, and therefore I pray, Madam, do not part with us.'

The rough old man walked to the dais and kissed Christina's hand. As he turned he took a dirty rag from his pocket and wiped away his tears.

For the first time that morning the Queen's face softened and as she watched the old man return to his seat her eyes were gentle.

When she turned to the Master of Ceremonies and ordered him to read the long and formal Declaration of Abdication to the assembly, her voice was almost breaking.

There remained only the business of discussing the financial provisions of the declaration. The Diet cut down considerably her demands, but she still managed to obtain revenues which were far in excess of what the economy of Sweden could really bear.

There were members of the Clergy and of the highly devout peasants who vociferously insisted that these revenues would be paid only if she remained in Sweden.

Opposition to this proposal came from an unusual quarter. Charles Gustavus, under the pretext of allowing his cousin the freedom she desired, insisted that she be allowed to leave if that was her wish.

Perhaps only Christina realized that his new motive was to get rid of her so that she represented no potential danger to him when he was King. This was an unfamiliar Charles Gustavus, and one that she hardly understood.

By midday it was all over, and the Queen was escorted back to her apartments.

On 6 June the final scene was enacted. Once again in the lofty old hall of the castle Christina entered in full regalia, followed immediately by the King Elect.

While the Act of Abdication was read and put in front of her to sign, the Crown's Officers of the Realm placed the crown on her head and gave her the sceptre and golden orb to hold. The Sword of State and the Keys of the Kingdom lay on cushions beside her.

The moment came when the Queen died and a King was born.

The ceremonial had been carefully rehearsed but Count Brahe at the last moment refused to walk forward and remove the crown from her head. Christina gave him a look of hatred and removed it herself.

She stood up and took off the Royal cloak of purple.

It was immediately seized by a score of Members of the Diet, who rushed forward and grabbed it. Christina stood like a statue while they quarrelled over it and ripped it to pieces to obtain a souvenir.

Above the hubbub, wearing a dress of plain white silk, she made her speech of farewell.

After again repeating that she had tried to do her best for her country and asserting that she had done nothing for which she could reproach herself, she made a brief and cold speech about the qualities of the new King.

Oxenstierna, who should have made a reply, kept his resolve to take no part in the ceremonial. A minor Member of the Estates acted for him.

Charles Gustavus found in the hysteria of the moment that his old affection for Christina had returned. He began a fervid plea that she would undo all that had been done, and reascend the throne.

Suddenly realizing at length the absurdity of what he was saying, he rushed through his prepared speech, promising to be the servant of his people, and finally led Christina personally to her rooms.

'Stay with me,' she begged him, clinging to him with an intensity which he knew only too well was born of an inner desperation.

'You better than anyone else, know what I have to do now,' Charles replied.

Gently he disengaged himself from her hands which tried to hold him and moved away from her with what seemed to her overwrought senses to be a new pomposity.

She spent the rest of that day prostrate on her bed. The old nervous exhaustion, which made her body almost rigid, had returned.

Dimly she heard the bells of the old Cathedral ringing and soon there came the crash of cannon firing a salute.

The Coronation of Charles Gustavus was taking place – a simple and quick ceremony without spectacle or expense.

The reign of Queen Christina had come to an end.

CHAPTER NINE

ON the evening of the day that Christina abdicated a State Banquet had been arranged and the new King sent a personal request that she should attend.

Christina had no desire to be present at a function where she was no longer the main character, but she made one last effort to focus the limelight on herself.

She sent word to King Charles that she would be pleased to attend the feast provided she had a seat second only in importance to his own.

Knowing that her infatuated cousin would do anything to please her, she felt confident that this request would be granted.

She then told her valet that she did not intend to wear any special dress for the occasion, but she ordered him to fetch a pair of scissors. When he returned with them, she commanded him to cut her hair as short as a boy's.

The valet was dumbfounded because Christina's tresses were the most attractive part of her appearance.

'Cut them off,' she ordered. 'I have given away a Kingdom; I certainly do not mind losing my natural crown.'

The effect of her shorn head was all that she could desire.

She arrived late at the banqueting hall where everyone was already standing beside the tables, not daring to sit down until the King gave the order, and this he obviously had no intention of doing until Christina was present.

A buzz of excitement ran among the guests when they saw her at the door, and she smiled at them disdainfully. The King went over to her and escorted her to her seat.

The banquet then began, but Christina was something of a skeleton at the feast for everyone was embarrassed and even the King could not persuade her into conversation.

When he finally resigned himself to eating the meal in silence, Christina pushed her platter away from her, and suddenly demanded to know what arrangements he had made for her journey from Sweden.

'I have ordered twelve of our best warships to be ready for instant sailing tomorrow,' he replied. 'My captains have orders to show you every deference as a member of the Royal House of Vasa.'

Christina nodded with satisfaction, and then asked a series of questions about the transport of her books and art treasures.

She found that her cousin had seen to every detail. Having satisfied herself on these points, she arose and left the banquet without a word of apology or farewell.

It was a wet and stormy night, and as soon as she reached her own apartments, she scribbled a message which she handed to a servant, commanding him to give it to the King the following morning.

In this she explained briefly that because of the weather she had decided that she would not want the ships after all.

She then called her secretary and told him to bring some pistols, a carbine and the shabbiest men's clothes he could find. Within an hour she was on her way from Uppsala, riding on horseback and escorted by only five gentlemen.

They were headed by Steinberg, who had been promoted to the rank of Count and held the position of Master of the Queen's Horse, though in practice he was Christina's secretary.

The nobles hated this upstart intellectual because of his unswerving loyalty to his mistress and because he showed no inclination to feather his own nest from the privileges that went with his title.

The most notorious of Christina's one-time favourites, Count Magnus, had been greatly admired for obtaining four palaces and estates which brought him a personal income of 80,000 rix dollars a year.

Hundreds of titles conferred for favours given or to obtain urgently needed finances had sent the budget deficit soaring to four millions – four times as great as it had been ten years earlier.

But this draining of the lifeblood of the country did not unduly worry the nobles who personally gained from the situation.

What they could not understand or tolerate was a man who showed no venality.

Steinberg had in fact received his grandiose reward for saving Christina from drowning. One morning at four o'clock she had suddenly insisted on inspecting a new warship.

The obese old Admiral Herman Fleming was hastily dragged out of bed to conduct the Queen over the ship. Half asleep and unable to see properly in the half light he slipped on the gangplank, put out his hands and involuntarily dragged the Queen with him.

Steinberg immediately dived in and rescued Christina, bringing her ashore without her dress or petticoats which the Admiral had pulled off in his frantic attempts to avoid drowning.

Christina made no fuss whatever about the incident at the time, but that evening she privately made her rescuer a Count.

For once she had chosen well. Steinberg's loyalty was never in question in the long years that he served her.

He was the kind of man who was content to worship his idol from afar. With unusual wisdom Christina had confided to no one but him the route from Sweden that she was taking.

The remaining four men in the party were insignificant but reasonably honest. They had been commanded by the King to obey Christina without question, and they rode in fatalistic resignation behind her through the pouring rain.

She reached Stockholm long after midnight and spent the following day writing letters to various friends abroad. She also had a long interview with a goldsmith about an expensive medallion which she wanted to be struck to commemorate her abdication.

At twilight she set out again for the South, huge crowds lining the road out of the town, and with the cannon of the fortresses firing the salutes she loved so much. She made a detour to Nyköping in order to pay a last visit to her mother.

On this occasion the interview was exceedingly brief, and Christina did all the talking.

The Queen Mother, now ageing, was ill and for once had nothing to say. In fact she was so thunderstruck at her daughter's quixotic activities that she could not even summon up the usual hysterical outburst.

Christina was with her little more than half an hour and as she had not slept for twenty-four hours, she spent the rest of that day in bed.

She lay down in the male attire that she had worn since she started from Uppsala, and the fact that she had been constantly soaked by rain brought on a severe cold.

Although she resumed her journey on the following morning, the cold turned to pleurisy and she was compelled to stop for a week at a farmhouse.

There she insisted that she was the son of Count Dohna, although the farmer and his wife knew perfectly well that she was the ex-Queen.

When she arrived at the little port of Helsinborg she was weak and still seriously ill.

On the quayside Baron Linde handed her a letter from the King. In it Charles made a sincere appeal to her to change her mind and marry him. Christina read it and then said to the Baron:

'You know the contents of this letter?'

The Baron replied that the King had confided in him a brief outline of it.

'Then tell my cousin,' Christina said to the Count, 'that I might have married him with better grace while I was still on the throne. His Majesty should remember that the crown is a prettier girl than I, and that now he is married to it. I am sure that the King is prudent enough to rule without my advice, and certainly I see no other reason why he should desire me at his bed and board.'

Without any formality she then embarked on a small ship for the short crossing to Denmark.

The delays on her journey through Sweden had permitted the news of her imminent arrival in the Danish kingdom to get ahead, and she had all the crowds she desired to greet her as she stepped ashore at Elsinore.

But her reception at the Danish Court was decidedly cool, partly because she was no longer a Queen, and also for the reason that Denmark was most anxious not to upset her powerful neighbour.

The Swedish Government had sent spies to watch Christina.

They sent back varying reports, some slanderous, some sensational, some entirely imaginary, but on one thing they were all unanimous – that the Queen was now making no secret of the fact that she intended to become a Catholic.

In the Estates at Stockholm, the horrified clergy demanded that her income should be reduced if the reports were true, while the peasants and nobles agreed that something must be done to curb her extravagance.

Christina attempted to buy popularity by making ostentatious gifts to almost every man and woman that she met.

Finding Denmark hostile, she soon crossed the border, and on 10 July reached Hamburg. She rode into the city dressed like a cavalier with a red scarf round her neck.

Her friend, Antonio Pimentelli – the Spanish Ambassador who had gone ahead to arrange her reception in Europe – had advised her months before to contact one of the richest Jewish financiers in the country, a man named Texeira, a refugee from Portugal.

The Jew, who was not accustomed to any regard from the aristocracy, was delighted when Christina imperiously demanded that she should be his guest.

At dinner that night she gave him a full and frank account of her financial affairs, and although they were already in complete chaos, this experienced moneylender realized that whatever she did, Sweden was not likely to allow their ex-Queen to become completely penniless.

He regarded her as a reasonable security for a loan and a still better political investment.

'At the same time, my Lady,' he added, thoughtfully fingering his beard, 'you must decide quickly either to deny or confirm the rumours of your conversion. As a Jew, it is no concern of mine as to what branch of the Christian belief you adopt, but it is as well to remember that the people of your country may well make certain moves to your financial detriment should you become a Catholic.'

Christina began to retort angrily that she was her own mistress and would do as she liked. But Texeira interrupted her.

'This I accept and I see no reason why you should not announce the decision I now realize you have already made. You must never forget that the new King is in love with you, and you will be able to obtain money simply because of this, provided, of course, that you never make him your enemy.'

Christina saw the force of the Jew's remarks and promptly asked for writing material. She then scribbled the first of many flattering letters which were to maintain her income largely without interruption for years to come.

The Queen decided to remain in Texeira's house, paying him a nominal rental.

She was far better received in Hamburg than she had been

in Denmark, and on the Jew's advice she behaved with more propriety than in the past, wearing women's clothes again and conducting herself with some dignity.

On 30 July, however, she became bored and shortly before midnight put on her boy's clothes once again and set out for the Netherlands, ordering the considerable retinue that she had by this time collected to make their way there as best they could.

She rode with her escorting gentlemen in a leisurely fashion seeing the sights and calling without warning at the castles of surprised aristocrats where she expected to be received with all the ceremony due to a person of Royal blood.

At one point near Munster she visited a Jesuit college, and being taken by the monk on duty at the door to be a man, she was admitted.

She was conducted to the Reverend Father and highly embarrassed the devout old man by making ribald suggestions about the morals and mode of living of the student monks under his care.

One or two of the newer members had heard in the outside world about Christina's liking for masculine disguise and they had seen some of the numerous sketches of her which illustrated the flood of slanderous pamphlets which were in existence.

They guessed that the boisterous young man who wandered everywhere about the college was, in fact, the notorious Queen, but they were too terrified to say so until after she had left.

The next day Christina sent her secretary with a gift of one hundred ducats which mollified the Reverend Father, and he made no official complaint about her disgraceful behaviour.

On 12 August she arrived in Antwerp, where she put up in the house of a rich merchant who was a business friend of Texeira's. This she turned into a miniature palace, receiving the Archduke Leopold and various other notable personalities in full state.

She thoroughly enjoyed her stay in the city, where a wide variety of amusements were prepared for her, but she also made serious preparations in secret for her conversion.

The agents who still shadowed her every movement learned all about the messages which she sent to Rome, and they were duly reported to Stockholm.

They proved a death blow to Oxenstierna, who had still obstinately believed that the little girl he had loved and the grown woman he had feared would never in fact take this terrible step.

He had often boasted that the worst catastrophes of war had not upset him.

The death of Gustavus Adolphus and the defeat of the Swedish army at Nördlingen were, he said, the only two occasions when he had had a sleepless night. But this treachery of a Vasa to the religion for which the family had fought and died, killed him.

Christina heard the news of his death early in September, just as she was preparing to attend a firework display arranged in her honour. She went just the same. Her mother's death a few months later did, however, upset her. For three weeks she cut out all amusements.

In December she announced that her preparations for her journey to Brussels were complete.

She travelled by water in a barge which was decorated above the water-line with gold, and armed with twelve pieces of cannon. A dozen horses drew the barge in relays.

She approached Brussels late in the afternoon, as darkness was falling. The city was illuminated by hundreds of bonfires outside the walls, and by thousands of troops holding torches on the walls themselves.

Over the main gate a set-piece had been erected which showed two angels holding a laurel leaf with the name 'Christina' on it.

By the time she had disembarked it was past midnight, but the streets were still crammed with curious onlookers. In fact, nobody could have slept for the inevitable cannon were firing their salutes and every church bell in the city was ringing its welcome.

Despite the slush of snow which had fallen earlier, carpets had been laid along the streets which led to the Archduke's Palace, and Christina walked along them bowing with delight at her reception and pausing so often so that she could be admired that it was past two o'clock in the morning when she greeted the Archduke.

She was so excited that she refused to go to bed and walked restlessly about the Palace to find windows from which she could see the still illuminated city.

She complained petulantly when, at dawn, the torches disappeared and the bonfires died down.

Later that day, in the private chapel of the Palace, she made her secret profession of the Catholic faith. It was, according to her, a secret one, because she had still not completely organized her financial matters with Sweden.

But the secrecy was somewhat nullified because she arranged for cannon to fire at the precise moment when she was given absolution. Naturally everybody in the city demanded to know why the cannon had begun firing again.

Christina had created all the notoriety she could possibly desire, yet she felt desperately rootless.

Her conversion was ostensibly a private matter, and Rome ordered the delay of any public celebrations until she made a more formal profession of faith.

She was thus officially neither Lutheran nor Catholic, and probably never in her life did she so vehemently desire to identify herself with some religion.

She longed to be reassured by a priest that, even if her ways were mysterious, God understood them. And without this help either from the creed of her birth or from her future Church, she sought to quieten her uneasy conscience by indulging in a whirl of amusements which gave no time for thought.

The Archduke did his best for her, arranging dances, tournaments and hunting parties which Christina apparently enjoyed. But in the quietness of her room, when she rose as usual long before the winter's dawn, her sense of frustration returned with redoubled force.

She felt homesick and bereft of those whom she had loved and who she wanted to believe had loved her.

It was at this time that her mental reserve broke down and she poured out her heart to Ebba Sparre, living her pleasant life as a member of the La Gardie family and adulated as 'the Beautiful Countess' throughout Sweden.

'How supreme would be my good fortune if I could share it with you,' she wrote, 'and if you could see my happiness. I assure you that the gods might envy me if I could only have the joy of seeing you.

'But as I cannot have this satisfaction I can only pray that you will believe that wherever I am in this world I shall treasure your precious memory and that over there, beyond the mountains, I shall carry with me the passion and tenderness I have always felt for you.

'Keep me at least in your dear memory, and do not spoil by forgetfulness the happiness of the one being in all the world who honours you the most. Adieu, my Belle; remember your Christina.'

She re-read the words as she scattered the sand over the wet ink.

Already she was half regretting the frankness of her letter, and wondering if the shallow Ebba would allow other eyes to see her beseeching plea.

With an attempt at bravado she added a postscript to deny any insinuation of unhappiness that Ebba's husband might read between the lines.

'Give my compliments to all my friends, male and female, even to those who do not wish to be friendly to me. I forgive them with all my heart, all the more because I am none the worse for them.

'I forgot to tell you that I am perfectly well and receive untold honours; I get along well with everybody, except the Prince of Condé, whom I never see except at the play or on the hunting field.

'My occupations are to eat well and sleep well, to study a little, talk, laugh and go to the plays, and to pass the time pleasantly. In short, I listen to no more sermons; I despise all orators, in accordance with Solomon's precept that all is vanity, and everyone should eat, drink and be merry.'

The final words were indeed the truth. The weeks sped by in interminable merrymaking – most of it at Christina's expense. She was at one and the same time eager to make a spectacular gesture in token of her new beliefs and yet hesitated to take the plunge.

Circumstances which delayed the next step and the patient policy of Rome, which counted a century as of little account in the journey to Truth, gave her all the excuses she needed to put off any major move.

She contented herself by forecasting something really sensational when the time came.

When the news reached Stockholm that Christina was

planning to make a public statement of her conversion, the new King was deeply worried, not only because of the political repercussions that might occur, but because he feared that the Estates, urged on by the clergy, would deprive her of her revenues.

He decided to make one last appeal to her either to return to Sweden, or to abandon her plans, by sending as an emissary a young man whom he knew she particularly liked.

This was Count Tott, and the King's choice showed how impersonal were his efforts on behalf of Christina, for the Count had at one time been accounted a serious rival to Charles Gustavus for the young Queen's affections.

The Estates would never have permitted Tott to leave the country if they had not been told that the real reason for the Count's journey was to inform Christina of the King's proposed marriage to Hedwig Eleanora of Holstein.

The message stressed the fact that this was a political marriage, and that the King still hoped against hope that he could abandon it if only Christina would give up her plans and accept his hand in marriage.

Count Tott had an audience with Christina and stated the King's views.

She was quite unimpressed and he then told her with brutal frankness of the general feeling in Sweden, stressing that she was in very real danger of being reduced to complete poverty. Christina angrily refused to change her mind.

'I gave up a throne so that I could have freedom,' she told him. 'The Swedish people forget that they did not give me the crown; I inherited it as a Vasa. Just as I had a right to it by birth, I have also a right to renounce it should I so desire.'

She then dismissed Tott, who remained in Flanders for a little time but received no further summons to her presence.

Nevertheless, Christina was considerably disturbed by all that she had heard, and, unknown to Tott, she sent a letter by her secretary, Steinberg, to the King repeating her certainty that he would always have a regard for her as she had for him.

She begged him to continue their friendship and to look after her financial interests. She told him that all the scandalous rumours about her moral conduct were false.

But in the letter she neither wished him well for his marriage, nor made any mention of her conversion to the Catholic religion.

One reason for the delay in arranging her public profession of faith was the death of Pope Innocent X on 7 January, 1655. The election of the new Pope Alexander VII did not take place until April.

All this time Christina impatiently awaited a message to say that she would be welcome in Rome.

Soon after the new Pope ascended the throne he wrote her a letter assuring her that, immediately she had made a public profession of her faith, the whole Catholic world would show their satisfaction by welcoming her as no other convert had ever been welcomed.

Christina was delighted with the news and immediately began her plans for a spectacular progress through Europe.

She started to pledge her credit so that she could purchase all sorts of presents for her acquaintances, and order new and expensive equipment for her journey. The news of her lavish spending attracted a motley crowd of adventurers to her retinue.

At her request, Antonio Pimentelli, who had been quietly awaiting his summons in the Low Countries, was appointed the Spanish delegate to her suite and he was the only person of importance in it.

In his turn he attracted a number of people prominent in Spanish politics, which disturbed not only the Swedish Government but French political circles as well.

The rest of the company who gathered at her house during the summertime preparations, numbering nearly two hundred with only five women among them, had no particular liking for Christina, but simply thought that they could have a luxurious time as members of her entourage.

They set out from Brussels in September. The journey provided little excitement except that on the way Christina paid a visit to the exiled King Charles II of England.

The monarch-in-exile had been profoundly disturbed by Christina's change of attitude to the Stuarts shortly after the English revolution.

At first, the example of Cromwell had seemed a dangerous one to her, and she had dabbled with the idea of sending some sort of aid to Charles I simply to prove the basic loyalties of reigning houses and in particular to curb any aspirations of

Oxenstierna, who with some reason she sometimes imagined might emulate the Protector of England.

Later she admired the mailed-fist policy of Cromwell and was wholeheartedly on his side, often saying that if he had any sense he would declare himself King.

Her regard for the Commonwealth and its leader was increased when Sir Bulstrode Whitelocke arrived in Stockholm as the English Ambassador. He was a Puritan, getting on in years, and had a limp.

Christina looked on him as a wise old uncle, and although he was shocked by her behaviour and coarse language, he allowed his pity to conquer his anger.

The Queen never forgot his placid, ever-just attitude during the crisis of her abdication, and the Commonwealth of England remained in her mind as a friendly country – a possible haven and an assured ally.

All this Charles Stuart well knew. He also recognized that both the Queen and he were incurable romanticists.

Always on the alert for an intriguing woman or a useful conspirator he had looked forward greatly to his meeting with her. His sentiments were amply reciprocated.

When they met in 1655 any idea of matrimony – a thought that had at one time crossed both their minds – was, of course, a thing of the past, but they had a delightful *tête-à-tête* when for more than two hours each boasted of their amatory conquests.

But Charles was too astute a man to ally himself with a woman who he realized at this meeting was little more than a curiosity.

Apart from giving the Queen the courtesy of personally watching her procession resume the journey, he made no special gesture towards her.

Late in October Christina reached the Alps.

In a little mountain village she met Father Malines, the priest who had come in secret to Stockholm and learned of her intention to embrace Catholicism. He was now the personal envoy of the Pope, and gave her instructions about her behaviour at the coming ceremony.

She arrived in Innsbruck on 1 November, and two days later everything was ready for her public profession.

The Papal authorities had arranged a spectacular service and the Archduke called for Christina at the house where she was staying. She had been ordered to dress in black, but she insisted on wearing an enormous and rather vulgar crucifix on her breast, which sparkled with five huge diamonds obtained for her by Texeira.

On foot she walked through the gaily decorated streets to the Cathedral, followed by a long procession of nobles and officials of the Church. She made her declaration in an over-loud voice and was then given absolution.

She sat perfectly quietly through the sermon which was based on the text:

'Hearken, O daughter, and incline thine eyes; forget also thine own people and thy father's house.'

Then she signed four copies of her profession of faith and the service was over.

The rest of the day became a celebration with the usual cannon salutes, fireworks and bonfires. In the evening a musical comedy, which had been specially written for the occasion, was the highlight of the entertainment.

As the distinguished audience took their places Christina astonished those around her by exclaiming in a loud voice:

'It is but right, gentlemen, that you should treat me to a comedy since this morning I treated you to a farce.'

There was complete silence after she made this remarkable statement, but she seemed utterly unaware of the embarrassment that she was causing, for she was deep in conversation with Pimentelli and hardly troubled to look at the actors on the stage.

The next day Christina impatiently demanded to know how soon she could proceed to Rome. She was told that some time would have to pass before the arrangements could be completed. But at last, in bitter December weather, the cavalcade set off.

One reason for the delay was a financial crisis, but the ever-helpful Texeira temporarily solved her problems by arranging a large loan at an exorbitant interest.

The procession which left Innsbruck was several hundred yards long, Christina at the head, for she insisted on travelling on horseback rather than in the ostentatious coach which she had bought.

Most of the towns she passed through greeted her with great pomp and ceremony, having been ordered to do so by Rome, but there were exceptions.

The Venetian Republic pretended that there was an outbreak of plague in the districts through which Christina passed and refused to entertain her.

Some distance from Rome the Pope sent a special coach for her, and as the weather was by now very bad, she changed from her horse and travelled in this until she neared the Holy City.

Christina arrived in Rome on 19 December, late in the evening.

On being introduced to the Pope, she threw herself prone on the ground and kissed his toe. He took her by the hand and escorted her to a throne covered in crimson velvet and had a brief talk with her, being careful to keep all doors wide open.

He explained that she had rather upset the arrangements he had made to welcome her because it was expected that she would wait outside the city until a formal invitation was sent her.

Rather petulantly she agreed to behave decorously and keep herself out of sight until she received permission to make a public entry.

On 23 December, 1655, she was told that everything was ready, and she left the town secretly and went to an inn where she changed into a costume which she had designed as being typical of an Amazon.

Mounted on a white horse, she then rode at the head of her procession through lines of troops and immense crowds to the great square in front of St. Peter's.

There the priests conducted her to the Pope's chapel, where she was confirmed, taking the name of Alexandria as a compliment to the Pope himself and to the great warrior King whom she admired and considered herself to be remarkably like both in character and ability.

On that day Christina behaved as well as the Papal authorities could desire, but the excitement of the subsequent celebrations soon banished her propriety.

When she attended daily Mass, she often giggled and talked even through the most solemn parts of the service.

The Pope, hearing of her activities which shocked both the congregation and the officiating priests, sent her a rosary with an exhortation that she should use it while she attended Mass to keep her mind off worldly things. Christina took the rosary, examined its worth, and then threw it on a table:

'I did not become a Catholic to tell beads,' she told the horrified emissary.

Christina could not complain about the immediate and tangible advantages that accrued from her conversion.

The noble Farnese palace, only a century old and bearing the stamp of Michelangelo's artistic genius, was placed at her disposal by the Duke of Parma.

Magnificent as was the exterior, it was around the lovely courtyard and in the lofty rooms that its real treasures stood. Decorative paintings of priceless value were the background for peerless examples of classical and contemporary art.

Christina headed her suite as they swarmed into the building. She walked through room after room furnished to the last detail and providing her with every comfort, both physical and intellectual.

She was overcome with merriment when she saw that the nude statues had been modestly swathed in draperies. One of the first things she did was personally to tear these emblems of modesty away.

She also essayed one or two bawdy remarks on the subject but even she sensed that her humour was ill-timed and for a while she was silent as she looked on examples of art about which hitherto she had only read in books.

Forgotten now were the crates of her own treasures which lay in the warehouses of Antwerp, awaiting her orders.

All she demanded should be sent on were the most valuable of her books for which room could be found in the huge Farnese library.

Invitations flooded in. Hitherto Christina had rarely ignored the opportunity to enjoy herself in company, but there was something about the quiet serenity of the salons of the Farnese Palace which attracted her even more than the excitement of balls and masquerades.

For hour after hour she would shut herself in a room, walking round and round soaking herself in its luxury and beauty.

It was at such a time that her thoughts sped once more to the one person who could make this peacefulness perfect.

Temporarily at least her desire for the tantalizing attraction of Pimentelli, and her hunger for heady dalliance with some doubtful and low-born hanger-on in her retinue, were banished.

She remembered the fleeting happiness which had almost been in her grasp time after time in her adolescence.

Once again she longed for Ebba, and although there had been no reply to her earlier letter, she once again unburdened her heart to the indifferent Countess.

'How happy I could be, could I see you, Belle,' she wrote, 'but I am condemned to the hard fate of loving you from a distance; the envy the stars have of human happiness prevents me from being entirely happy myself while I am separated from you.

'Wherever I am in this world there will always be someone entirely yours as I have been always. Is it possible, Belle, that you remember me? Am I as dear as I always used to be to you? Was I not rather mistaken when I persuaded myself that I was the person you loved best in the world?

'Ah, if that be so, then leave me my illusion! Do not undeceive me; then neither time nor absence shall deprive me of it. Adieu, Belle. I kiss you a million times.'

She knew in her heart that Ebba had never really loved her but she hoped against hope for a reply.

Christina's inevitable reaction to her new mode of life was not long delayed. She tried to escape from a growing sense of unhappiness by filling every hour of the day and night with activity.

Sensitive to the fact that she was no longer a reigning Queen, she attempted to create notoriety for herself by gaucherie and contemptuous manners.

Every woman who was not of Royal blood was forbidden to sit in her presence, and Christina deliberately kept them on their feet until some of the less robust ladies, weighed down by their heavy costumes, fainted from fatigue.

Male guests, by contrast, were treated as equals whatever their lineage or background.

Gradually the visits of the best families ceased, but the gaps were more than filled by the mob of rogues and charlatans who found it both amusing and profitable to make themselves welcome in the Farnese Palace.

Antonio Pimentelli, like Count Magnus before him, discovered that his coldly calculated plans to enslave Christina by toying with her emotions began to go awry. He had spent valuable months in making love to her and in gaining her confidence.

And on the journey to Rome he reasonably thought that a long campaign which had involved activities which even the most enthusiastic diplomat might have regarded as beyond the call of duty, was nearing the triumph which would permit his return to a more normal life.

But he had to accept the situation that Christina had merely used him as an amusing toy for her desires and a useful tool for her ambitions.

She greeted the Spaniard and his colleagues with increasing coldness and one day insulted them by forcing the resignation of Don Antonio de Cueva, a prominent Spanish general who had accompanied Antonio Pimentelli from Flanders, saying:

'I intend henceforth to have only gentlemen in my suite.'

She also told innumerable people that if Cueva had not been a personal friend of the King of Spain she would have had him horsewhipped.

The insult was the greater when the identity of one of the new gentlemen became known.

On the way to Rome, Count Francesco Santinelli, a young ne'er-do-well, whose principal social asset was a lithe long body which looked magnificent when he performed a solo dance of his own devising, had attached himself to the procession.

Principally through his terpsichorean abilities plus a ready talent to compose extempore verse, Christina had invited him to reside with her. Rather to his surprise, but certainly to his deep satisfaction, he found himself in de Cueva's post.

He decided to mark and learn his predecessor's sins and profit from the lesson.

All that Antonio de Cueva had done was to report some of Christina's activities to the Spanish faction in Rome. Christina did not mind these tantalizing accounts in the slightest, but they did give her a chance to strengthen her position with France, for she was taking more and more interest in the glamorous Court of Versailles.

The Spaniards were not the only people in Rome who were beginning to wish that Christina with her retinue would resume her wanderings to France or anywhere else that tempted her.

The Pope heard daily that all was not as it should be at the Farnese Palace.

The standard of gentlemanly behaviour of which Christina boasted took unusual forms. The major-domo left by the

Duke of Parma to look after the residence during Christina's tenancy spent most of the time hiding in his room for the ex-Queen's servants had a habit of attacking him if he made any inspection of the premises.

An Italian rogue named the Marquis Giovanni Rinaldo de Monaldeschi, who had been appointed Grand Equerry by Christina simply because of his flashing eyes and gallant ways, was one man who made no secret of the motives he felt in allying himself with Christina's cause, whatever that might be.

He saw the chance of loot, financial embezzlement and protection for his own private and usually reprehensible adventures.

Monaldeschi gave the less courageous gang who had appointed themselves to various vaguely defined posts on Christina's staff the example they desired.

The Italian Marquis had an excellent and practical knowledge of art; he was able to select the most valuable ornaments in the Palace for them to sell.

Under his discriminating eye some skilful smiths ripped off gold and silver ornamentation and artfully replaced it with copper and iron. He found seamstresses who could repair the marks where over-enthusiastic knives had slashed tapestries from their settings.

He deprecated, but did not stop, the tearing down of bed curtains, door hangings and the pilfering of small and almost valueless mats.

He had made most careful arrangements to receive a percentage of the profits made when anything was stolen.

It did not matter whether the sale was a pleasantly long negotiation with some ambitious and quite conscienceless Roman parvenu or whether it brought in a few ducats from haggling in a second-hand street market.

Christina turned a blind eye to these goings-on.

Even when autumn brought a chill to the evenings and she saw the remains of a richly carved door burning merrily in the grate she made no protest at vandalism which did, in fact, horrify her.

She knew that there was no money for fuel just as there was no money for her servants' wages. By virtually permitting them to sack the palace she solved for the time being her immediate financial problems. Almost every penny had disappeared.

She had been robbed, flattered into making extravagant gifts, fleeced by crooks of all kinds who flocked to sell her forged masterpieces and valueless bric-à-brac.

She was more deeply worried about finances than she liked to admit even to herself.

The new King of Sweden had taken the easy way out of his most pressing economic problems: when the ghastly state of the national exchequer from Christina's extravagances became fully known, he went to war.

Sweden had marched on Poland, and then found Russia was also her enemy.

Whatever superficial benefits the change-over to a war economy provided for the grumbling peasants and more vociferously complaining nobles, Christina, whose sole virtue as a Queen had been her loathing of war as a permanent political policy, knew that her income was now in jeopardy.

Frantic messages to Texeira produced something to satisfy the most pressing creditors. But the Jewish financier told Christina that he did not think much of her plan to sell all her rights in the Crown lands assigned to her by the Swedish Estates in return for a lump sum.

As he pointed out, the King of Sweden himself was busily looking for purchasers of Crown lands, and Christina's possessions would be a drug on an overloaded market.

Christina, who had been indulging in uncharacteristic excesses of eating and drinking at the exotic banquets which Rome's culinary experts and vintners prepared in her honour, now found her physical health deteriorating.

On top of the ill-advised dietary regime, she was again exhausting herself in the familiar pursuit of culture.

Even if she ignored the Papal plea of a little more public profession of her faith – 'Better an Ave Maria before the world than a thousand private prayers,' the Pope told his disappointing convert – she was striving madly to justify a reputation as the Sibyl from the North.

Her garden parties gave her the pretext to organize a society which was eventually known as the Arcadian Academy.

There was a certain flavour of the old Order of Aramanta about it in that each member took the name of an Arcadian shepherd or shepherdess, and there was an expensive brooch as an emblem of membership.

The aims were, however, entirely commendable and innocent.

Christina kept her more amusing activities for the evenings. The culture by day and the fun by night were the last extra burdens both her body and brain found insupportable. She became seriously ill.

The Pope sent the best doctors in the Vatican to attend her, and when she recovered he agreed wholeheartedly with the suggestion that a change would do her good.

In truth, the Holy Father had become heartily tired of the interminable reports of Christina's behaviour and he wanted time to think.

Couriers were sent to smooth the way for Christina to visit France. The difficulties of finance were temporarily relieved by a loan from the Papal treasury of 20,000 crowns, while Christina pawned most of her jewellery for a further 10,000 crowns.

To her delight she was told that one of the Pope's private galleys would be placed at her disposal for the passage to Marseilles.

The official preparations for her journey went through with remarkable smoothness and celerity.

One of the most alarming rumours about Christina's amours had been suddenly revived – and with such circumstantial evidence that it could no longer be dismissed as a tavern anecdote.

The Pope had appointed the young and brilliant Cardinal Dezio Azzolini to bring some sort of order into Christina's household.

He was an aristocrat who had adopted an ecclesiastical career at an early age and his rise had been meteoric. By the time he was thirty-one he was a Cardinal, and he had been the strong influence in the election of Alexander as Pope less than a year before.

Extremely handsome, with a delicately curved mouth, long sensitive fingers, and a subtle, dexterous wit, Dezio Azzolini would have attracted any woman, let alone the susceptible Christina, yet this was the man who the Holy Father believed implicitly could restore virtue to the Farnese Palace.

As soon as Cardinal Azzolini arrived and put a stop to the most blatant excesses of Christina's retinue the outwitted rogues not unnaturally began a campaign of slander.

The Pope took no notice of it beyond asking – and receiving –

Azzolini's assurance that his relationship with Christina was merely official and entirely innocent.

For a time the rumours died down. Then, during Christina's convalescence they began again – and from a different source.

The tavern talk was a belated echo of the ominous stories which were reported to the Papal authorities by dignitaries of the city who were shocked rather than intrigued.

The Pope, with all the knowledge of human frailty that his high office gave him, prayed that time and distance would prevent this exasperating young woman from destroying the reputation and career of one of the most capable men in the Vatican.

The Holy Father was, in fact, determined that somehow he would save young Azzolini's career. He was too young to suffer as poor old Cardinal Colonna had done.

Well in his fifties and with a face like dried parchment from overlong studies in arid libraries, the elderly prelate had been so moonstruck by the enticing Christina that he had begun to use rouge on his cheeks, and when he imagined that the Queen was beginning to look with favour on him, he threw all discretion to the winds.

With a shudder Alexander recalled a most reliable report that the Cardinal, dressed as a wandering troubadour, could be seen any night beneath Christina's bedroom window, serenading her in a cracked voice and plucking an execrable tune from a lyre.

Colonna had been banished from Rome to end his days away from temptation in the obscure safety of a minor monastery.

Now the Pope began to wonder if the tinkling laughter that had been reported from the bedroom while Colonna sang was not merely amusement at the clown below but disgraceful evidence of the ex-Queen's amatory pleasures on which a scandalous jingle had been based.

Alexander pondered on the distasteful words he had insisted on hearing from the embarrassed agent.

'Now her dear Azzolini in Rome
So charmed her with delight
From him she could not live a day
Nor pass a tedious night.'

He had decided at that moment that Christina's departure

from Rome would have to be treated as a matter of great urgency.

Cardinal Azzolini was not in attendance when Christina stepped aboard the Papal galley at Civita Vecchia.

But it was seen that she was clasping a locket on a chain to her bosom as she paid her respects to the aged Cardinals who had been chosen to bid her godspeed. Inside was a miniature of Azzolini.

As the vessel moved out to sea she kept to her curtained cabin.

Not even Monaldeschi or Santinelli, who were accompanying her, could persuade her to come out and enjoy the sea air.

She was in a delightful reverie, reliving wild moments of love – and passion.

CHAPTER TEN

As the Papal galley crawled along the coast, Christina asked to put in at Frejus, the port on the Mediterranean coast of South-Eastern France where Julius Caesar landed his troops for the conquest of Gaul.

She admired the Roman Emperor almost as much as she venerated Alexander the Great, and she felt it would be a significant act to enter France in the steps of her hero. But the galley commander had strict orders from the Pope.

Her request was ignored and the galley, leading three smaller vessels which had been sent to add some measure of majesty to the ex-Queen's shabby retinue, sailed on westwards.

At Marseilles the Duc de Guise, Grand Chamberlain of France, was deputed to welcome Christina in the name of the King.

He awaited her in full robes of State, bored with a duty which had occasioned a tiresome journey and a protracted stay at Marseilles.

He was not impressed by this much-talked-about woman of a remote Scandinavian reigning family, who now had nothing left but the unimpressive aura of Royal birth.

And he was determined to make her realize that, even though she was the ward of a member of one of France's noblest families, she was fortunate to be the guest of the greatest nation in Europe.

Christina, however, ignored his slightly condescending attitude and the instant she was on shore talked animatedly to him about her project to march on Naples.

The Duc could find nothing to say, but his sense of humour eventually asserted itself and he told his retinue that the journey to Paris might be amusing.

Once again Christina's bizarre attitude to life – and to men – had attracted a man whose emotional palate had long been jaded.

An hour before she arrived the Grand Chamberlain would have insisted that there were no tricks of Eve which could still enthrall him.

But, as the Queen stared at him indifferently and cursed the heat with a string of oaths that reminded him of his jailers in that embarrassing period when he had languished in prison for political sins, he eyed her with fascination rather than curiosity.

The Duc's first high hopes were more than fulfilled on the journey northwards. Christina treated him as if she were another man. She talked to him with disarming frankness about her own ideas of amusement and demanded to know of his own in return.

Try as he would he could not entirely maintain the stiff and lifeless attitude which was his usual method of defence against the world around him.

Between the towns where formal receptions had been organized he and Christina, both on horseback, would often gallop far ahead of the procession.

At other times they would fall far behind their retinue, to the consternation of the officers and troops of the cavalry escort.

The Duc's delight in the guest he had been told to bring to Court as slowly as possible was, at least for the early part of the journey, merely that of an observer. He was intrigued by her lack of femininity but not attracted by it.

He preferred to study her mind and heart as mystifying examples of the twisting tricks Nature could play in the eternal game of sex.

Depravity he had known, and love and lust in a thousand different disguises. But his cynicism made him assert that sex was the motive for every motion and that men and women had no deeper yearnings than those which could be satisfied by the indulgence of their bodies.

His study of the frailties of mankind had, however, not dulled his curiosity, and his interest in Christina was deepened when, with extraordinary outspokenness, she told him of her adventure when they stopped at Lyons for two days.

After the ceremony of welcome the travellers were left alone to rest and amuse themselves as they would.

Christina, ever interested in the new world she was invading, did not trouble to change her man's clothes before she left the house placed at her disposal by a side door and began wandering about the town without an escort.

All Lyons knew, of course, that Royal troops escorting a distinguished visitor were in the town. The streets were decorated and everyone was enjoying the evening breezes down by the river, taking a cup of wine and gossiping about the remarkable woman who had ridden through the city gates on horseback.

Christina wandered among the crowds, listening with delight to the often lewd comments she overheard about herself.

Along the river bank, where the boys and girls of the town made their trysts, she suddenly caught her breath at the sight of a girl who was walking slowly towards her.

She was fair – the first fair-haired girl Christina had seen among these swarthy Latins. And she bore an uncanny resemblance to Ebba.

The Queen got into conversation with her.

The girl knew that this person with a harsh French accent must be one of the visitors, and was flattered at the attention she was receiving.

'You are very lovely,' Christina said.

'There are many girls in Lyons to whom you could say the same,' the girl answered.

Christina took her hand and kissed it and the girl giggled. Just as Ebba had giggled and simpered long ago.

The Queen drew the girl closer to her; they were now in a less-frequented part of the river, and any passers-by were too used to young lovers to give them more than a passing glance.

Christina kissed the girl's cheek. There were ineffective little murmurs of protest, flirtatiously inviting more until her mouth found two softly parted lips.

In a long passionate possessive kiss she drew the girl's slim body closer and closer until there was a sudden cry of horror.

The girl had realized that it was a woman's body pressed against hers. She tried to pull herself away, while Christina rained kisses on her mouth, her eyes and her neck.

'No, no, stay with me,' she pleaded. 'You are so sweet, so lovely, I love you.'

The girl began to fight like a frightened cat until Christina was forced to let her go. Then, gathering up her skirts, she ran, screaming invectives, back to the safety of the busy town. A few lovers eyed the scene with mild interest.

Christina had the sense to accept defeat. She melted into the gathering shadows of evening and returned to her house.

There she recounted her adventure to the Duc, continually overcome by mirth and yet obviously proud of the duplicity that had almost convinced the girl of Lyons that she was a man.

The Duc sat smiling enigmatically, watching the brightness of her eyes, and the quick excitement which stirred her breasts beneath the plain masculinity of her coat.

'It would have been so amusing to have carried the matter to the end,' Christina concluded regretfully. 'Tell me, Your Grace, if I had not returned and, searching you had found me in some bawdy house with this little trollop in my arms, what would you have said?'

The Duc smiled. He was well aware that Christina was endeavouring to startle, if not to shock him.

His studies of human nature made him understand all too well that her desire to recapture her own sensations by talking of them was mixed with an ambition to appear sexually dashing and successful.

It was a combination that was almost universal among many young men. The only unique part about it in this case was that the *raconteuse* was a woman.

He began to think that perhaps the stories which were whispered of the Queen's physical abnormalities might have some foundation in truth.

The Duc had heard of Ebba Sparre. And he noticed the meticulous description Christina had given of the French girl's fair hair and blue eyes.

Then he saw in the Queen's eyes just a momentary glimpse of agony before it was banished by her merriment and loud laugh. His heart went out to her at that moment.

He too knew what it meant to be alone in a world crowded with people.

Mental heart-searchings had long since banished from his mind the fraudulent pretence that in physical love this loneliness could be destroyed.

He knew that it was a hydra-headed monster that returned in redoubled intensity on the wings of the dawn after the close intimacies of the night. And he was sensitive enough to understand that in a neurotic highly sexed woman the yearning for love was impossible to assuage and unnatural to deny.

The Duc de Guise slept but little that night. He had retired early, refusing Christina's invitation to sit a while in company with Giovanni Monaldeschi and herself.

He lay in his bed wondering what they were doing. Then he looked into himself – and what he saw slightly alarmed him. He suspected that he was falling in love.

When the journey was resumed he treated Christina with a new and real deference. There was, too, a closer intimacy in their conversation.

Christina recognized the significance of the change. She bloomed into a woman of charm. Her boisterous behaviour was softened by a sense of coquetry. Instinctively she responded to the gallantry in the Duc's eyes, the magnetism he exuded and which was unmistakably a challenge.

Christina's reception in France was all that she could desire. Louis XIV and Cardinal Mazarin had given orders to every town on the road between Marseilles and Paris to greet her with all the adulation usually deserved by a reigning Queen.

The reason for this policy was that Christina had conceived a fantastic idea of becoming Queen of Naples.

In the changeable conditions of European politics at that time the French Government could not rule out the possibility that she would achieve her object.

France and Christina had much the same interests in this idea. Both wanted to score a point off Spain, and both were eager to change the regime in Naples.

Christina also thought that it was an excellent method of obtaining some money, for she knew that France still owed Sweden vast sums from the alliance during the Thirty Years War.

She imagined that at least part of this sum could be obtained to finance the expeditionary force which she would lead. She told Giovanni Monaldeschi:

'My greatest ambition is to see a large battle, and I am determined that one day I shall take part in one. You will be my field-marshal.'

Giovanni had little desire to take part in any dangerous soldiering, but he too believed that Christina might succeed in her plot, and he spent much of his time in France intriguing with French statesmen to obtain both financial and military support for the project.

Louis, wary of offending the Swedish Government, was able

to pay his country's respects to Christina by treating her as a monarch, which thereby minimized the importance attached to her as a convert to the Catholic faith.

The magnificent coach which had been provided for Christina rumbled empty along the dusty roads of France during a very warm autumn while the Queen galloped beside the Grand Chamberlain. At one point Bourdelot came to see her and joined the little procession as far as Paris.

The Duc continued to be fascinated by Christina's personality. He told a friend of his what she was really like:

'Her arms are beautiful,' he said. 'Her hands, as large as a man's, are white and well-formed. One of her shoulders is a little higher than the other, but it is not really noticeable. She has a hawk-like nose and a large but pleasant mouth. Her teeth are fair. Her eyes are beautiful and full of fire.

'She pulls her bodice so tightly that it looks almost like a man's doublet, and she wears men's dress. The best way to flatter her is to tell her that she looks just like a man, and she has repeatedly said that she intends the people of France to remember her as an Amazon.'

Christina reached Fontainebleau on 4 September.

She was met by Mlle. de Montpensier, La Grande Demoiselle of the French Court, who was so struck by her appearance that she made a record of her impressions that evening:

'I had so often heard of the Swedish Queen's strange way of dressing that I was dying with fear lest I should laugh when I caught sight of her, but when I perceived her she surprised me very much but I did not want to laugh.

She wore a grey petticoat laced with gold and silver, a close-fitting jacket the colour of fire with lace to match her petticoat, a lace handkerchief round her neck tied with flaming red ribbon, a blonde wig with a knot behind, and a hat with black feathers which she carried in her hand.

'She is very fair, with blue eyes which are sometimes very soft, but at others very bold, a pleasing though large mouth, fine teeth, large nose. She is very small, her bad figure hidden by her jacket. The general effect is that of a pretty little boy.'

Later Mlle. de Montpensier was horrified by Christina's unconventional behaviour, for, within a few hours of her arrival, the Queen was swearing in almost every sentence and sprawling on the gilt chairs.

The ladies who had come to be introduced with her sat primly shocked at this peculiar visitor they had been ordered to treat with the greatest courtesy.

Naturally, all of them advanced, curtseyed, and wanted to kiss her either on the cheek or on the hand, according to their own social position.

Christina giggled at this courtesy and demanded in a loud voice:

'What makes all these ladies so anxious to kiss me? Is it because I am like a man?'

She remained at Fontainebleau until 8 September, when she was told that the City of Paris was ready to welcome her. She made the short journey mounted on a white horse, in a dress of brilliant scarlet and carrying her feathered hat.

A thousand cavalry men escorted her. Enormous crowds had turned out to see her. They lined the road from the town walls as far as Notre Dame, where she impatiently endured a brief service.

A carriage took her to the apartments which had been set aside for her in the Louvre, and for the rest of that day and all through the next, she held court to many notable Parisians as well as visitors to the city, among them being Queen Henrietta of England.

The French Royal family was at this time at Compiègne, and Christina was impatient to see the French King and also the most powerful woman in Europe, his mother, Anne of Austria.

As a matter of fact, Louis was as eager to see Christina as she was to talk to him, and he had earlier come incognito to one of her receptions.

He returned to Compiègne to tell his mother that he was most intrigued with their Royal visitor, but his rosy description of her charm was not borne out when Christina arrived at Compiègne.

She had been so impatient to get there that she had rejected all suggestions that she should stop a short distance from the Palace and tidy herself. As a result, she was covered in dust and utterly weary as she stepped from her carriage.

Those around her commented that she looked rather like an itinerant gypsy.

Nevertheless, anxious to be well regarded, she was for some days on her very best behaviour, and the Royal Family was impressed both with her perfect command of the French language and the profound knowledge she seemed to have of all the leading families of France.

But the good impression rapidly disappeared as Christina reverted to her real self.

At times she was more haughty than the Queen Mother herself, at others she was so rude about the attempts to entertain her that plans were put in hand to get rid of her as soon as possible.

Typical of her ill-mannered attitude was her reaction while she watched a deeply tragic play with a religious theme enacted by Jesuits. She roared with laughter the whole time.

After the performance a Father of the Order, who was the King's Confessor, sought an opportunity gently to reprimand her, but she said mockingly:

'I would be sorry to have Jesuits as my enemies for I know they are strong, but I would be equally sorry to have them either as my confessors or my actors.'

After a fortnight's stay at Compiègne, Christina left to visit Ninon de l'Enclos, who was staying at Senlis.

For years she had admired Ninon from afar. Chanut, Bourdelot, members of the French embassies in Stockholm and Rome, and anyone who had ever been in Paris, were badgered by her to recount all the anecdotes they knew about the most attractive woman in Europe.

Then when they praised the famous courtesan for her brains, her beauty, and her sacrifices on the altar of Venus, Christina would fly into a violent temper and demand that they cease to talk about her.

In actual fact Ninon de l'Enclos was the only woman in the world Christina admired. Born ten years before the Queen she was the daughter of an obscure officer of Touraine.

Like Christina, she had an unhappy childhood. At fifteen she was an orphan – her assets a small inheritance, a remarkable brain, and unsurpassed beauty.

Ninon's chestnut hair, luminous hazel eyes, creamy skin, and almost childlike figure were the means of attracting men so that she rapidly became the most adored woman in France.

But it was her brain that chained her lovers to her until she was the supreme power behind the scenes of French literature and art.

Probably no woman in history has ever been so completely

the mistress of her own emotions. Love was her life, yet she never trampled on its beauty by taking tangible rewards for her favours.

Indeed, none of the scores of men on whom she bestowed her charms until she was over eighty – and still beautiful – were expected to pay for the happiness, advice and instruction she gave them.

Ninon de l'Enclos was a queen among women, and Christina knew it. She envied this commoner her Royal prerogative as she envied nothing else on earth.

Deliberately she refused to allow anyone to accompany her when she visited the Venus of France. And Ninon, discreet and kindly as was her wont, never revealed what passed between them.

It is certain that she helped Christina to grapple with the problems which tore at her soul. And she would have stressed, as she stressed to other women, that love need not be lasting. She was a hedonist, catching the fleeting pleasures of the hour.

Yet she never had a lover unless she was passionately fond of him.

If Christina had asked the question that was always in her mind – the question of love and marriage (and doubtless she did ask it) Ninon would have told her:

'A woman should never take a lover without the consent of her heart, nor a husband without the concurrence of her reason.'

The pattern of Christina's life from the time of that afternoon's conversation in the tiny house at Senlis indicated that she had listened to such a view and had found no fault in it.

By this time the Queen had outstayed her welcome in France. The invitations to her to continue her journey elsewhere were so pointed that she could not possibly refuse, but she was completely penniless.

The various people who had trailed behind her on the way to Paris had, as they saw the money disappearing, fallen away one by one on the journey northwards.

Even Christina's white horse had been sold without her knowledge. Only Monaldeschi and a valet remained.

Louis sent her two rather shabby coaches which any tradesman in Paris could have hired, and the money to pay for them for a week's journey. He gratuitously insulted her by refraining from sending any gift as a memento of her visit.

Christina did not seem to have realized how great had been her failure to ingratiate herself with the French Court. But she knew by now that her dreams of leading an army which would battle their way south so as to put her on the throne of Naples had come to nothing.

She made a leisurely journey across France, this time without any celebrations in the towns through which she passed. She crossed the Alps and stopped in Turin, where she heard that plague was raging in Rome.

The rest revived her recently lost hopes about aid from France, and she ordered Giovanni Monaldeschi to return to Paris to see what he could do.

The Italian went, but made no great effort to carry out his orders, contenting himself with enjoying the hospitality of numerous friends to whom he recounted piquant and intimate anecdotes about Christina.

Alone, Christina moved to Pesaro, where she spent her time writing long letters to Cardinal Azzolini in Rome. She had a sudden longing for him, for his gaiety, his brilliance – his love.

'The days pass like centuries, because I am not close to you,' she wrote, and meant it.

CHAPTER ELEVEN

THE plague in Rome appeared to be strangely protracted and virulent.

Christina's inquiries as to whether it would be safe to return were answered from the Vatican with dire warnings of the danger.

There were also fervent pleas that she should safeguard her health, which she suspected were not entirely disinterested.

'Alexander thinks more of his finances than the souls under his care,' she protested to her valet.

The Pope, like so many of the Church of Rome adherents, looked on Christina as an interesting capture – rather like a savage animal which intrigues the onlooker but causes endless worry to its keeper.

Alexander VII had strict views on the need for economy. He would tell every visitor to the Vatican of his cuts in minor expenditures, citing the fact that he had used the same pen for two years.

He rarely talked of the large-scale financial retrenchments he had made which infuriated the Roman money-lenders but strengthened the Papal economy.

The debts with the highest interest had all been redeemed soon after he became the Vicar of Christ, and all the rest were reorganized at the unheard-of low interest of four per cent.

He disliked the pomp and ceremony of his office, preferring when the weather was fine the quiet of his country estates, while during the winter months he spent hours investigating the genealogical trees of the leading families of Europe and arranging his coin collection.

There was little common ground between such a man and Christina.

She became very bored. There was nothing to occupy her mind in the turgid provincialism of Pesaro.

She was still physically infatuated with Giovanni Monaldeschi but he was in France. The affectionate letters which passed between them almost daily were a poor consolation for her loneliness.

She sought in her imagination for new excitements, found none, and harked back to the Naples project. When she had landed at Marseilles this had been a somewhat vague dream.

Although France officially let her know that unless she could meet them three-quarters of the way the possibility of military and financial help was remote, she had wheedled out of the Duc de Guise certain information.

This, in retrospect, made the picture somewhat rosier.

The Duc and Christina were kindred spirits in their love for power, and he had been able to tell her from first-hand knowledge of the violent changes of fate and fortune which an able manipulator could achieve on the fiery Neapolitans.

'The rule of Naples once depended on a basket of peaches,' he told her as they rode together. 'The Spanish authorities in control of the kingdom put a tax on fruit, which was endured until the carts arrived at the city gates with the first peaches.

'The peasants refused to pay the dues, and when troops came to enforce order they were driven off under a hail of peaches. Even the Viceroy had to take refuge in a monastery to avoid the missiles.

'When I say that you as a Queen could attain the loyal love of these people I assure you that is no exaggeration. After the battle of the peaches a young fish hawker named Aniello took charge.

'He invited every brigand for miles around to join his force and soon had 10,000 Neapolitans under his command. In a matter of hours he was the real king of Naples. Naturally the common fellow hadn't the slightest conception of his duties. He walked about in a ridiculous suit of golden armour, ordering executions by the hundred a day.'

The Duc de Guise would have liked to describe the appalling atrocities in detail. He decided, however, such horrors were not for a woman's ears, even one as masculine inclined as Christina.

He, like many other people, had no idea of the latent sadistic streak in her contradictory character.

'Power had sent Aniello mad,' he continued, 'and quite rightly Spain had him assassinated, but to illustrate the fierce love that these Neapolitans can feel for someone who takes the trouble to lead them are the stories that the mob put his dis-membered body together and rounded up four thousand priests to conduct his funeral.

'And to this day there isn't a man, woman or child in Naples who does not believe that in the midst of the obsequies the head became adhered to the trunk, the eyes opened and a voice emerged in a great roar from the lips.'

'You have a remarkable knowledge of all this,' said Christina.

'I happened to be arranging a divorce in Rome at the time,' the Duc explained, 'and as my ancestors once owned Southern Italy it seemed to me reasonable that I should help these people by ruling them. I sent emissaries to acquaint the Neapolitans with my decision.

'I rather feel that their enthusiasm was not on account of my own undoubted talents to rule but simply because they would have accepted anybody who was not Spanish.'

'What happened?' Christina asked.

'It was an amusing experience,' the Duc continued, 'for I had to lodge for a time with a peculiar fellow who was a gun-smith and had succeeded the unfortunate Aniello. They were most devoted subjects after I was proclaimed Duke of the Neapolitan Republic, and I will admit I thoroughly enjoyed myself for a few weeks.

'But I hadn't any money and found it impossible to bribe my way through the crisis when Spain decided to get rid of me. They put me in prison – an unfortunate occurrence which you, my dear Christina, would I hope avoid.'

Christina vividly recalled this story as she languished in Pesaro. She thought she saw with great clarity how she could profit by the Duc's mistakes. One of them was his failure to obtain French soldiers and French gold.

Accordingly she sent Santinelli off to Paris to see what Giovanni Monaldeschi was up to and to start some political intrigues himself.

Santinelli, with the object of scoring off his rival, prepared some unfavourable but veracious reports on Monaldeschi's activities, and concentrated on ingratiating himself with Mazarin.

The great Cardinal, able successor to the tradition of Richelieu, was a gambler by instinct and origin. He had not been unimpressed by Christina, and as he had climbed to power on the shoulders of a woman – Anne of Austria – he favoured the idea of increasing his influence through another woman.

He told Francesco Santinelli that his mistress's plans were not by any means so impossible as he may have suggested at their earlier meeting, but he insisted on patience. The time was not ripe.

Meantime, he was pleased to make Christina a small and private gift of fifteen thousand crowns.

The one quality Christina lacked above all others was patience. The gift convinced her that Mazarin was only waiting for her to make a definite move. She announced that she was returning to France as soon as she could organize the journey.

Mazarin's couriers hurried to her to state that her presence would not be acceptable in Paris. But they suggested she might find Avignon a pleasant resting place until times were more appropriate.

Christina refused to take the hint and started to move northwards. Etiquette forced the French Court to assign her rooms at Fontainebleau.

It was a safe distance from Compiègne where Louis was in residence.

Christina arrived in October.

Santinelli had earlier been sent from France to Rome where he embezzled Christina's few remaining valuables which had been stored in the Farnese Palace.

Giovanni Monaldeschi obeyed her peremptory commands to leave his Parisian cronies and return to her retinue.

When he arrived he tried, as soon as they were alone, to embrace her. She repulsed him because she saw in his face that the rumours she had tried to dismiss were true.

Monaldeschi's degeneracy had not only coarsened his affections so that even the tolerant Christina felt revolted in the very presence of a man she had once considered the most handsome and charming of her gallants; it had also blunted his intelligence.

He did not see that to traduce the intimate confidences she had made to him spelt terrible danger.

He started to strut around the pathetic little court which Christina set up in the deserted palace of Fontainebleau and to enjoy himself in every possible excess with the perverts he brought from Paris.

He dabbled in the political intrigues which he fomented by

pretending to play a more personal part in Christina's Neapolitan schemes and in her influence over the Vatican than was in fact the truth.

Christina watched and waited. Ostensibly she spent her days designing uniforms for her Neapolitan expeditionary force, and supervising the making of the decorative jack-boots she herself intended to wear on the campaign.

But all the time she watched her erstwhile lover. She paid ostlers and tavern-keepers, agents and discarded mistresses, with jewels and trinkets for information on his activities.

She lowered her customary dignity in order to meet this riff-raff in person and hear their stories from their own lips.

Corrupt and perfidious himself, Monaldeschi rejected the idea that others could outwit his cunning. He went on his way in blissful expectation of his future power.

He treated Christina with such formal veneration that his every word and gesture became an insulting travesty of the courtesy and ritualistic obeisance they purported to be.

He failed to see that when Christina looked at him, there was a growing anger not far from murder in her eyes.

He had never loved Christina, but he had desired her as he desired every woman with whom he came in contact. In her surrender he revelled in the knowledge that a Queen was his, but such self-satisfaction was a poor substitute for the thrills that new affairs could provide.

With the typical vanity of the born seducer he imagined that just as no woman could resist him so no woman could tire of him.

Christina, he felt confident, would emerge from her temporary coldness the moment she had no other emotional distraction.

Monaldeschi had arranged a number of quite pleasurable meetings with one of the maids who cleaned Christina's bedroom. The girl was only thirteen but remarkably intelligent.

As she was illiterate it had been perfectly safe to persuade her to bring any scraps of paper thrown away beside the desk where Christina was wont to sit at four o'clock in the morning when she could not sleep.

The servant girl brought plenty of rubbish to her trysts – sketches of uniforms, calculations about money, scrawled and inaccurate maps for the invasion of Naples.

But a few pieces confirmed to Monaldeschi what he had suspected – Santinelli was so constantly in Christina's thoughts that he himself was being forced to take second place.

The rivalry of Giovanni Monaldeschi and Francesco Santinelli had grown steadily because for a long time Christina bestowed her favours equally on both.

Monaldeschi thought that the opportunity to outwit the Italian adventurer was timely when Santinelli remained in Rome.

He began preparing a diabolical scheme to ensure that Christina would banish his rival from her Court.

What exactly he wrote in the letters which he prepared remains unknown, but it is fairly certain that he made doubly sure by recounting both her private activities and her schemes for political power.

Christina had always been suspicious of everyone around her, and she made a strange rule that even their most private correspondence had to be shown to her if she requested to see it.

Where she thought the rule was being disobeyed, she used to probe in the personal belongings of everyone from her secretary to the humblest maid. Monaldeschi knew this, and he was, therefore, fairly confident that if he left letters incriminating Santinelli lying about they would soon be seen.

Unfortunately for his plans Christina was not so gullible as he expected her to be.

She found the letters, read them, and realized they had not been written by Santinelli. It was not difficult for her to guess who was interested in incriminating the absent man.

She had Monaldeschi's rooms searched and found letters written by him which exceeded in treachery anything he had attempted to foist on Santinelli.

One morning in October, 1657 Christina told Monaldeschi that she suspected one of her most intimate friends was guilty of betraying her secrets.

'I don't doubt that you know who I mean,' she ended.

Monaldeschi felt asured that his plot had succeeded, and he said:

'If you have been betrayed it can be by no other than the person absent from your retinue. There cannot be any forgiveness for such perfidy.'

'I agree with you,' Christina replied. 'What does a man deserve who betrays me in this way?'

'He should be put to death, and I offer myself to be executioner or victim,' he boasted insolently.

He had absolute confidence that by his challenge he proved his own loyalty. Christina had a peculiar look in her eyes as she nodded agreement.

'I am glad you say this,' she told him. 'Remember your words. I promise you I will not pardon such a traitor.'

When Monaldeschi had left her, she again read through the letters she had found in his room. She made copies of them in her own writing, then carefully wrapped them up, both the originals and the copies, and sealed them.

She sent a messenger to fetch the Prior of the Maturins, who was living in the Palace at Fontainebleau, and who acted as her confessor.

When he arrived, Christina handed him the sealed packet and told him to take good care of it until she asked him for it again.

For the next three weeks she arranged that all letters to Monaldeschi should be intercepted.

When he realized that his correspondence was being tampered with, he became frightened and devised several provisional plans to get out of France if an emergency arose.

But his vanity still made him believe that he was safe because of the circumstantial evidence he had built up against Santinelli.

On 10 November the crisis came – too late for him to flee.

He was told that the Queen wished to see him, and he went to the Galerie des Cerfs, which formed part of the apartments which Christina occupied in the Palace.

A summons so early in the morning was unusual, and at the last moment he had a dreadful foreboding that his plans must have miscarried.

He came to Christina not as the proud lover she had known for so many months, nor as the insolent courtier of recent weeks, but as a pale and trembling coward.

She spoke to him with deceptive politeness, commenting on trivialities such as the weather and her plans for the day, until a door at the far end of the gallery opened and the Prior entered.

Monaldeschi was alarmed to note that the door behind the Prelate was closed by an unseen hand. He looked round and saw that the entrance he himself had used was now guarded by three soldiers.

Christina's face had darkened. She held out her hand to the Prior for the sealed packet he had brought with him. She broke the seals and handed Monaldeschi the copies she had made of his letters.

He looked at them and in answer to her demands as to whether he recognized the contents, said:

'The writing is your own.'

'So you haven't any knowledge of these letters?' Christina demanded.

Monaldeschi, who was trembling and was scarcely able to control his voice, replied:

'How can I? They are forgeries.'

He still hoped that bluff could save him from a plot which seemed to have got completely out of control. He refused to believe that he could be hoist with his own petard.

She remained silent for a time, hoping against hope that he would say something more, for she still believed that he might be able to deny the treachery which the letters seemingly proved.

When he did not speak she took the original letters from the packet and showed them to him without letting him take them from her hand.

Monaldeschi did not need to look very closely; they were in his own writing.

He began babbling excuses, trying to blame everybody with whom Christina had been intimate. When he saw the futility of this, he threw himself prostrate on the floor, attempting to grasp the Queen's ankles and kiss her feet.

Christina backed away and summoned the three soldiers to pull him erect and search him.

In his pockets were found some more letters, and when the Queen had quickly read through them, there was no longer any possibility of denying what he had done to her. She backed away from him in loathing.

Monaldeschi tore himself from the grip of the soldiers and ran stumbling to her side, begging her to listen to him. She kept her face averted but said nothing until the whining man ceased speaking from sheer exhaustion.

Christina then turned to the Prior.

'Father,' she demanded, 'be witness to the fact that I hurry nothing, but that I am giving this traitor more time than he can reasonably demand from his victim to prove his innocence – if that were possible.'

The Prior nodded but did not say anything. After Monaldeschi began babbling away again Christina impatiently thrust him aside with an ebony cane and went towards the door through which he had entered.

As she grasped the handle, she beckoned to the Prior:

'Father, I leave this man in your hands. Prepare him for his death.'

The Prior was dumbfounded at what was happening.

Although he had agreed to keep secret under the seal of the confessional all that was contained in the letters, he was horrified when he realized that Christina was preparing to take the matter of punishment into her own hands as if she were both judge and executioner.

He begged her to pardon the man, or at least allow him to have a proper trial.

'I cannot grant your request,' she answered coldly. 'A traitor is worse than the most wicked criminal whose body is broken on the wheel. This man that you now see shivering on the floor has been the recipient of my most intimate secrets and private thoughts.

'I have loaded him with benefits and I have given him my affection. I am not his executioner. His own conscience has sentenced him to death.'

She moved from the gallery, but left the door open in order that she could hear and glimpse all that was going on. Monaldeschi got up from the floor and tried to run after her.

The soldiers, who had drawn their swords, pressed the points against his body so that if he moved they would have run him through.

They had been given their orders and promised large rewards if they carried them out, but, having some semblance of decency in them, they found it impossible to kill the helpless man in cold blood.

One of them went to the door and asked the Queen to show mercy. She shook her head.

'You have your orders.'

The soldier came back and there was an unaccustomed kindness in his face as he said to Monaldeschi:

'Think upon your God and your soul, for you must die.'

The Prior then attempted to reason with Christina, and begged her in the name of the Saviour to show some pity. Christina, angry and almost hysterical, replied that Monaldeschi's black treachery could only be punished by death.

The Prior, realizing that his appeals on the consideration of Christian decency and humanity were having no result, solemnly warned her of the secular repercussions of her proposed action.

'Your Majesty must realize that you are a guest in the Palace of the King of France. You would be wise to reflect on the King's attitude in this matter.'

'The King of France is not lodging me here as a prisoner or an exile,' she answered proudly. 'I am an anointed Queen and I am mistress of my own will. I can do justice on my officers everywhere and always. To God alone am I accountable for my actions.'

'It is true that Monarchs have ordered summary executions,' the Prior said gently, 'but they have always been in their own kingdoms.'

He saw the flecks of spittle on Christina's lips as her rage and fury mounted at this reproof, and trying to calm her he continued:

Madam, it is by the honour and reputation that Your Majesty has acquired since she left Sweden, and by the hope that the Kingdom of France has conceived in her negotiations for the further adoption of power that I beg you humbly to consider that this action, just and reasonable as it may be from Your Majesty's point of view, can be regarded by others as violent and precipitate.

'Surely Your Majesty's reputation would be increased rather by an act of generosity and mercy towards this poor man.

'I beg you to place him in the hands of the King of France, where he will have the justice of a proper trial. You will then be able to add to your title the description of "Admirable".'

'Why should I be reduced to beg for justice against a traitor when I am in sovereign power over him?' Christina demanded. 'I hold the written proof of his treachery. Go back to him and pray for his soul. I have no intention of doing what you ask.'

The old priest returned to Monaldeschi and took the trembling man in his arms, telling him that he had done all he could.

Monaldeschi began shrieking and tried to begin a confession, but his moans made the words incoherent, and finally, not knowing what he was saying, he was in such a state of terror that he was shouting prayers in a mixture of Latin, French and Italian.

The soldiers, who were anxious to get their ghastly task completed, grew impatient at these ravings.

One of them dragged Monaldeschi roughly to his feet. Their prisoner staggered back until he came up against the wall. The soldier prodded his stomach with a sword.

Monaldeschi, terrified that this was the end, seized the blade with his hand. As the sword was pulled away, it cut off three fingers.

The executioner lunged at Monaldeschi's heart, but the ring of metal against metal showed that the Italian had suspected assassination and had put a coat of chain mail under his doublet.

The soldier then gave him a vicious slash across the face. With blood pouring from his cheek and a great pool forming on the floor where it pulsed from his mutilated hand, Monaldeschi subsided on the floor, half held up by the wall.

There the Prior gave him Absolution.

Through weakness from loss of blood and because his terror was reducing him to a coma, Monaldeschi fell forwards on his face. A second soldier slashed at his skull, splintering the bone.

The blow turned him over, and all three men began stabbing wherever the coat of chain mail did not protect the body.

Monaldeschi's mutilated hand moved up to his neck and, with the stumps of his fingers, he pointed to his throat, begging them with his eyes, for his mouth was now so full of blood that speech was impossible, to cut off his head.

His signs were ignored, and the soldiers continued to stab at him brutally until they were mutilating a corpse from which the life had already fled.

All the time this ghastly execution slowly reached its climax, Christina leaned against the wall just beyond the door.

She was unable to see what was going on, but the groans of the dying man, the curses of his executioners, and the prayers of the priest begging God for mercy for the dying victim, told her that her desire for revenge was being fulfilled.

When it was all over, she came back into the room and

looked coldly at the mutilated body of her lover. Imperiously she turned to the Prior:

'Take him away and bury him,' she ordered. 'I will send you two hundred livres so that you can have a Mass said for his black and unworthy soul.'

The horror and disgust of the French Court when the details of this affair became known shook even Christina's confidence in the righteousness of her action. The King saw to it that she learned that in the opinion of France she had committed murder.

From that awful day in November until February, she remained alone at Fontainebleau.

No member of the French Court was allowed to visit her and no invitation whatever came from any member of the French aristocracy to an entertainment, or even for her presence at the religious festivities at Christmas time.

Louis XIV was by tradition and personal character an autocratic monarch, but never had he or his ancestors performed summary justice of the kind that this Queen without a country thought it within her divine right to bestow.

All that Christina did to soften the indignation and disgust that her French hosts felt about the episode was dismiss the three soldiers who had carried out the execution.

They were glad to have an excuse to get out of France as quickly as possible and escape any belated arrest.

They had been well rewarded for their bloody work, and Christina secretly arranged for them to rejoin her as soon as she returned to Rome.

CHAPTER TWELVE

ONLY a nature hardened to the piercing shafts of innuendo and active dislike could have survived the ostracism which Christina had to endure after the murder of Giovanni Monaldeschi.

It must have been almost insupportable, even by a woman who expected to be misunderstood...

'Genius is a paradox to those who lack it,' Christina often said. And was convinced that it was not her fault that no one except herself regarded her ideas of justice as a mark of genius.

'Extraordinary merit is a crime never forgiven,' she remarked blithely to Cardinal Mazarin, who pretended not to hear.

He was the only person of note who deigned to meet her during those awful months in France which were the aftermath of the Fontainebleau tragedy. And he disciplined his mind to ignore the defects of behaviour in a woman who might possibly be of use to his country.

They both had need of each other and were prepared to compromise. Unfortunately Christina was no match for the wily statesman.

The war debts still owing by France to Sweden amounted to close on one million crowns. Mazarin said that he recognized Christina as a legitimate agent to collect them, but almost immediately he depressed her by adding that the best that the Treasury could do for the time being was to pay her an instalment of 33,000 crowns.

The Cardinal had carefully investigated the Queen's financial position and rightly estimated that she would not quibble on matters of principle when the tangible advantages of immediate payment were dangled before her. Christina, who was in the position of a beggar, was forced to accept with as good a grace as she could muster.

At the same time Mazarin started to ease Christina out of France. He did so by offering her the hospitality of his own small suite of rooms in the Louvre.

Depressed by her solitary and banal existence at Fontaine-bleau she was delighted, not seeing that the offer of accommodation meant for a commoner was really an insult to her Royal blood.

The Queen Mother, who was living in the main part of the vast old building, immediately announced her intention of deliberately ignoring the presence of the Swedish Amazon.

This strengthened the determination of French society to have nothing to do with Christina.

But the Queen's suite was relieved to get away from Fontainebleau because, despite the bitter January weather, the palace servants were, on orders, lighting no fires for them and there were even icicles inside the damp rooms.

One reason why Christina felt so happy about her sojourn in Paris was that it would give her a chance of fulfilling a long-held ambition to meet the celebrated members of the French Academy.

The savants were, however, much disturbed when a crate arrived one morning containing a badly executed portrait of the notorious Queen together with an imperious note which informed them that she intended to visit the Academy.

Many of the illustrious members had genuinely admired Christina's efforts to turn Stockholm into the Athens of the North and a few of them were ready to show their independence of mind by behaving in a manner contrary to the wishes of the King.

But the Monaldeschi murder was, to the majority, an incident which no amount of learning could extenuate.

An acrimonious discussion produced a solution of compromise. The members decided that trouble would be avoided by sending Christina an invitation to attend a routine evening session.

She arrived in a public carriage dressed in mannish clothes. She looked in vain for her portrait. It had not been hung.

She noted that only a dozen or so members had turned up to meet her and that they remained seated in her presence during a rather dreary session of poetry reading.

There was also a discussion on the de Chambre dictionary which was then in preparation. Some wit had left the page containing the word *Jeu* on the top of the pile of manuscripts. As an example of the word there was the sentence—

'Jeux des Princes qui ne plaisent qu'à ceux qui les font.'

('Amusements of princes which please only those who practise them.')

Christina coloured with anger as she read it, but passed the incident off with a mirthless laugh. She left the Academy a few minutes later.

The problem of somewhere to live was becoming acute. The Queen Mother – Anne of Austria – was putting more and more pressure on Cardinal Mazarin to get rid of this scandalous Swede.

A frantic scheme of Christina's to conquer fresh fields and inveigle Oliver Cromwell into inviting her to England came to nothing.

The Protector had sufficient troubles without creating more by playing host to a woman who believed implicitly in the Divine Right of Kings and was known to have a great admiration for the exiled Charles Stuart.

The only thing was to return to Rome, although Christina had considerable misgivings about the wisdom of this move, because the Farnese Palace was no longer available.

The decorators and furnishers were still busy on the repairs after the holocaust of her previous visit, and the Pope had not seen fit to report the end of the outbreak of plague, although everyone knew it had disappeared with the first cold of winter.

Cardinal Mazarin solved the matter for her.

After a stormy interview with the Queen Mother when she raged that either Christina left the Louvre or she did, Mazarin hurried to his troublesome guest and enticed her away with the offer of a French battle squadron to carry her to Rome.

'Italy is a warmer and kindlier country than France,' snapped Christina, 'but even there I shall require a roof over my head.'

'You can use my own palace,' said Mazarin resignedly.

He had hardly seen the place for years and there was very little in it to spoil.

He felt a cynical amusement as he realized that the gesture would arouse the suspicions of his Spanish enemies who might well see in his seeming friendship for the Queen a more vigorous support for her Naples project than was in fact the truth.

Mazarin never missed the opportunity of tweaking the nose of Castile.

The Cardinal omitted to tell Christina that the imposing

array of ships he had offered as an escort had to sail for Italy in any case to transport French troops for service under the Duke of Modena.

But because of these military requirements, the Queen had to make an awkward journey to Toulon, the military base for the expeditionary forces, and her departure from France was without ceremony or official farewell.

On the way the warlike atmosphere of the convoy aroused still further Christina's ambitions to ascend the throne of Naples.

As soon as the ships put into Leghorn she sought out the Duke of Modena and insisted on signing a treaty with him for mutual support in an invasion of Naples.

The Duke, who was ill, protested at the details of the agreement when Christina first presented him with the draft written in her own hand.

Then as he found resistance futile he insisted on adding precautionary clauses concerning the free passage of French troops through the Papal States.

This, added to the fact that the troops were to be recruited by Christina, made the agreement a scrap of useless paper.

The Queen, of course, ignored the almost impossible provisos, and hurried at her usual breakneck speed to Rome in order to persuade the Pope to grant the passage of the, so far, non-existent army.

It was the beginning of May, the weather was fine, and the day that a courier arrived reporting Christina's arrival in Italy His Holiness hurriedly left for his summer estates at Castel Gandolfo.

A gift of seasonable fruit and decorated meats awaited her in the hall of Cardinal Mazarin's palace, with a brief and formal message that they came with the compliments of the Pope.

Christina recognized that the present was a token of his refusal to meet her personally. Angrily she turned to the messenger who had brought it, and said:

'Thank the Pope for his gift. Clearly the Romans have little knowledge of the arts of war, for they supply the enemy with provisions before they lay siege to him.'

The siege began immediately – a menacing cordon around the Mazarin palace which kept Christina almost as isolated as she had been at Fontainebleau.

When she went out in the streets there were murmurs

among the crowd and often she heard the word 'murderess' as she passed.

It was noted that the detachment of the Papal Guard which escorted her on these outings made no attempts to belabour the culprits or to arrest the braver spirits who often ran alongside her carriage shaking their fists.

The mob was indeed merely giving expression to the sentiments held by everyone in Rome. The Monaldeschi execution was politically reprehensible, and evidently – for the Pope suggested no penitence – morally unforgivable.

The man whom Rome believed to have been the real culprit was Santinelli.

It was thought that he very adroitly risked punishment himself in providing circumstantial evidence for his rival Monaldeschi to use in the first of the tangled web of libellous correspondence, or else Christina was his infatuated dupe and had simply obeyed his suggestion for getting rid of a rival.

Santinelli pacified Christina in the besieged house with such pleasures and comforts as were within his power to provide.

There was no one else, for the Pope had deliberately kept Cardinal Azzolini close to his own side, believing that Satan had little chance when his intended victim was too busy to sin. Christina had to be content with writing notes to the man she longed to see.

These were necessarily formal because the only couriers available between the Papal household and her own were Vatican agents, and both she and Azzolini knew that their correspondence in either direction might be opened and read.

She passed the enervating months of a Roman summer in a state alternating between elation and depression.

At times she was able to enthuse over her plans for the Neapolitan campaign until all obstacles disappeared and she saw herself riding on a white charger through the gates of Naples, surrounded by the cheering populace.

These airy dreams, however, faded whenever a debt collector, with the persistency of his profession, forced his way into the Royal presence and made angry requests for payment.

Money once more became the most pressing worry, and more and more frequently the pleasing generalities of a military project had to be shelved while the practical problems of day-to-day existence were tackled.

In the autumn the news that her unenthusiastic ally the Duke of Modena had died came just as Christina was becoming rather bored with an idea which was so tiresomely complicated.

Characteristically she turned from the improbable to the impossible.

In faraway Constantinople an old lady was ruling an Empire through her grandson Mohammed IV and distinguishing the regime with atrocities which were horrifying even for the Ottoman Empire.

The Crescent cast a baleful light over Eastern Europe and Christians were being enslaved and massacred by the hundred in border skirmishes where infidels and Gentiles met.

It was to Santinelli, that willing but cynical listener, that Christina announced her latest idea.

'Christianity must start a Holy War,' she told him. 'I shall lead the Crusade – on a white horse – and with a costume quite different from that I had hoped to wear in the conquest of Naples.

'The first thing will be to form an alliance of every nation in Western Europe; the second to obtain loans to equip an international expeditionary force. You shall be my general.'

Santinelli murmured his gratitude at the honour but it was obvious that he was unenthusiastic about taking part in a campaign against an enemy who took no prisoners, or if they did, maintained their lives only so long as the tortures inflicted on them failed to bring death.

Christina was gradually getting tired of Santinelli. She talked no more to him about the project but found a sympathetic listener in the Venetian ambassador.

Venice had for some time been engaged in a desultory contest with Turkey for the possession of Crete, a vital point on the maritime trade route to the Orient.

The Republic's representative in Rome could not afford to ignore any scheme which might assist his country, even one as bizarre as Christina's, which she outlined with more and more excitement every time he was granted an audience.

Finally, however, warnings from the Pope, who by this time was keeping armed guards at the Mazarin Palace to check every visitor, had their effect.

The ambassador stayed away and Christina pigeon-holed the scheme along with the Neapolitan project.

She was, however, incapable of enduring a mental vacuum for very long.

Ambition consumed her, and paradoxically she fed on it. Somehow, she felt certain, she could attain power and solve her financial difficulties by a single effort.

The news from her own country provided her with a fresh inspiration. Sweden was in the midst of a war and experiencing many setbacks.

Christina's old loathing of military campaigning abroad as a Swedish political policy was revived because she knew that the man she hated most, Count Magnus de la Gardie, was the active fomenter of it and Charles the King his willing tool.

Once again Santinelli was invited to her private study to discuss military matters.

'I intend to offer myself as a field-marshal to the Elector of Brandenburg and lead his troops into Pomerania,' she told him.

'But that would be to wage war against your cousin and against Swedish troops,' Santinelli replied. He was appalled despite his own easy attitude to loyalty.

'Pomerania is a territory from which my revenues are supposed to come. It is overrun and I am not paid. Charles apparently cannot protect my territories. Therefore it will be both just and right that I should take matters into my own hands. I wonder if the Naples uniforms would be suitable . . .'

Christina went into one of her inevitable reveries about the appropriate dress for campaigning.

Santinelli left her to her thoughts. Accustomed as he was to her wild ideas, this one was really alarming, because the Elector was frantically looking for military help, and Christina's presence would undoubtedly be a formidable weapon against the morale of the Swedish troops.

It was a scheme that might well come off.

Santinelli was also worried because he had sold the Neapolitan uniforms, along with many of Christina's costumes of State and various trinkets he thought she would never miss. It would be ridiculous if his greater treacheries should come to light because of these minor embezzlements.

But fate was kind to him. Christina, blind to his venality and lack of brains, deputed him to be the emissary to explain her plan to the Elector in Vienna.

Immediately he heard this Santinelli purported to be

enthusiastic about the idea and assured her that he would be able to persuade the Elector to give her at least twenty thousand troops.

He left without making any preparations for his journey except to pawn everything he could lay his hands on and to bid a lasting farewell to his friends in Rome.

'I expect to be away for some time,' he averred with a wink.

So far as Christina was concerned, he had left Rome for ever. One or two brief notes of inquiry from her and empty promises on his part passed between Rome and Vienna.

Then Santinelli sank into the oblivion from which he had emerged.

Christina had another man to worship and comfort her; one for whom she had longed – Cardinal Azzolini was with her again. This almost unbelievable turn of events was something for which she had to thank the Pope.

Azzolini had worked unremittingly to heal the breach between Alexander and Christina.

'The Queen has learned many lessons in the past few months,' the Cardinal said persuasively. 'Everyone comments on how civil and docile she has become. She hasn't had a debt collector chased from the palace these past six weeks and she never goes out to entertainments which she knows Your Holiness would frown upon.'

'She is so impoverished that she dare not offend the debt collectors and she receives no invitations to entertainments,' the Pope replied.

'That is true, Your Holiness,' Azzolini agreed, 'though the poverty is no fault of hers. The Swedish King has broken his promises, and she is utterly without any source of income. But I think her quiet behaviour is due to the fact that she has reached the years of discretion. After all she is now a middle-aged woman – thirty-three this winter.'

'The age for woman's foolishness begins when she believes she is almost past it,' said the Pope. 'These Nordic women do not age as early as do those of Latin blood. And anyway the Queen's greatest charm is ageless.'

'Her greatest charm?' repeated Azzolini uncomfortably.

'Yes,' said the Pope, gently smiling. 'I cannot believe that you do not know that the – er – magnetism she exerts over your sex lies in her throat. Our poets talk of a musical bell-like voice as being the audible evidence of the wiles of Eve.

'They may be right, but certainly we must admit that the husky tone of the Swedish Queen is pleasing to the ear. I have noted the fact myself, even if the words she speaks have often annoyed me. I give you warning, my son, that there is the whisper of the Devil in that low, deep Nordic voice.'

Azzolini could find nothing to say. The Pope was right, of course. Christina, short and ungraceful, her large eyes blinking with short-sightedness, untidy and often unwashed, was not in any way attractive until she spoke.

Then the compelling quality of her voice, responding to her every mood no matter whether she was cursing or cajoling, captivated everyone who listened.

Alexander broke into Azzolini's thoughts. What he said amazed the Cardinal.

'Sometimes a gesture of conciliation can bring victory even if it symbolizes defeat,' he said slowly. 'The Queen is a precious child of the Church and we must hope that the burden of the years you mention are in truth bringing propriety. To help her I propose to let her live in the Riario Palace.

'It has been in disrepair and the decorations are of the simplest. Anyway, now that the most reprehensible of her entourage have – er – died or disappeared, the unfortunate troubles at the Farnese Palace are not likely to recur.'

'The palace will require more money for upkeep than she can find,' Cardinal Azzolini observed.

'I realize that, and I propose to grant her an income of 12,000 scudi a year. The Vatican finances are now stronger, and the money will be well spent.'

'I fear, indeed, it will be quickly spent,' the Cardinal sighed.

'I hope not, my son,' the Pope replied, 'for I am appointing you Controller of Her Majesty's Household.'

The Holy Father watched the Cardinal's reaction closely. In the young priest's face he saw all that he suspected. But he was still convinced that he had made the wisest – indeed the only possible – move.

Sometimes love can often be destroyed by proximity, especially if one of the lovers is an idealist.

Events proved that the Pope was wrong in this instance, but at least the scandal of the Queen's household was minimized.

Cardinal Azzolini took up his residence in the Riario Palace, engaged reliable servants, and in July, 1659 told Christina that she could move in as soon as she had swallowed her pride and craved an audience with the Pope.

She obeyed, receiving a short but frank homily and the Papal blessing.

There followed an almost unique period of serene happiness for her; the man she now worshipped was constantly by her side. His moderation and wisdom curbed both her quixotic bursts of acute depression and exhausting elation.

Under the Cardinal's tutelage the tangle of Christina's finances was turned into some semblance of order and she was able to examine her economic position objectively.

Even when it proved worse than she had even imagined, the realization did not really daunt her; Azzolini was there to find some way out of the impasse.

Slowly he eradicated from her mind her persecution complex, bidding her to study the events in Sweden before she claimed that the delays in payment of her revenues were nothing but a deliberately inflicted punishment for her abdication.

Cardinal Azzolini also calmed Christina's worst outburst of temper after she had read a letter from a friend in the Spanish Embassy about a woman who was exciting the Swedish countryside around Nörkoping by pretending to be the ex-Queen, travelling incognito.

The reason for this imposture was not discovered, and it is probable that the woman, whose name was Anne Gyldener, was just a crank.

She did, however, give an excellent imitation of Christina's behaviour, and, before she was arrested, managed to obtain large sums of money on credit, and enjoy herself enormously.

Christina was most anxious to know more about Anne Gyldener who, in appearance at least, deceived many people who had known her well.

She also wrongly suspected that there was some political intrigue behind the idea, possibly to arouse still further the hatred of the Swedish people and so facilitate a further cutting down of her often-delayed pension.

Christina, as it happened, completely misjudged her reputation with the Swedish people. Open-minded and honest herself, she had never bothered to organize any sort of secret service to keep her informed of the real situation in Sweden.

If she had done so, she might have learned that the story

that she was back in the country spread like wildfire and caused widespread rejoicing.

The commoners who had laughed derisively at Christina when she abdicated the throne, and had cheered Charles X to the echo, had learned bitter lessons in the six years that he had reigned.

At first his war policy had paid a spectacular dividend. The Vasa flag flew over Warsaw within two years of his accession.

But a year later the excesses of his troops had aroused the whole Polish nation and with Austrian aid Charles was soon fighting with his back to the Baltic and his claims on Prussia were abandoned.

It looked as if he would have to return to Stockholm and rule as a King in the King's Peace. If Christina had been his consort perhaps her loathing of Sweden's war policies would have made him acquiesce.

Certainly her intellectual dominance would have helped him successfully to undertake the task.

Without her Charles had neither the desire nor the ability to act as a statesman. He had become a hard and wooden-headed warrior, with little military skill but a tremendous amount of obstinate courage.

Instead of planning for peace he manoeuvred for wider hostilities. He cancelled the Estates' orders for an evacuation fleet to be sent so that his troops could retire to Sweden and demobilize, and marched on Holstein to attack Denmark.

Intense cold that winter enabled him to march across frozen rivers and maritime inlets and conquer the whole of Denmark.

The Great Powers forced him to abandon Denmark in return for territories in Danish sovereignty which thereby gave Sweden control of the Sound.

He signed the treaty in March, 1658, but five months later he again invaded Denmark without any declaration of war. For ten months his army rampaged over a worthless victim, for Copenhagen, the heart of the enemy country, held out.

As winter approached Charles found himself responsible for a starving army, with the knowledge that Brandenburg, Austria, and Poland were ranging forces to help Denmark, while England and France were bringing heavy diplomatic pressure to bear in order to force him to yield.

Charles's reply was to demand reinforcements from Stockholm. He was in the midst of his preparations for a renewal of hostilities when he became ill and died on 13 February, 1660.

The news reached the Riario Palace a week later, and Azzolini advised Christina to settle for once and for all her problems by visiting Sweden.

'The King's brother is now a Regent for your nephew, the infant King,' he said. 'I believe that he will be ready to discuss your finances sensibly and fairly. I advise you to ask him for permission to enter Sweden.'

'Ask permission!' demanded Christina angrily. 'You forget that I am a Queen . . .'

'A Queen who gave up her throne. It might be wise to show a conciliatory attitude. And you could be most useful as an adviser.' Seeing Christina's darkening face he went on hurriedly:

'The young King's education demands some thought. He is still a baby. We must hope that your own experiences as a child will not be repeated.'

'That is true,' Christina agreed. 'But I doubt whether my advice would be heeded. One of the Regency will be Magnus.'

Then at the thought of a chance to score off her old lover she laughed aloud.

'I'll go,' she cried.

She reached Hamburg in August, where she was told in no uncertain terms that the Swedish Government had no intention of welcoming her.

One of the members of the Regency was Count Brahe, an old friend of her father's, who, she hoped, still had some affection for her.

She wrote a letter to the Count saying that she had no desire to cause any disturbance, but believed that she could help in the financial crisis of the country by arranging some adjustment of her revenues.

She herself followed closely behind this letter, and by the time she reached Elsinore, an urgent note was awaiting her from Brahe begging her not to come any farther.

She ignored this, and persuaded the King of Denmark to send her in state aboard a Danish man-of-war to Helsinborg. No one was there to receive her when she landed.

She did in fact have to put guards on the door of her room in the inn where she stayed on arrival. She also learned that

Brahe was no longer her ally. Indeed, he hoped to find some excuse for imprisoning her at Aland.

As there was really no justification for such an action, emissaries were sent to beg Christina at least to stay away from Stockholm, where it was feared that Count Magnus and various cronies of his among the clergy would incite riots and possibly contrive her assassination.

Needless to say, Christina became impatient and ignored all these requests.

She rode on horseback into the capital as ostentatiously as possible, forgetting the advice Azzolini had given her.

The young King's mother, who was a rather foolish woman and quite ignorant of the political repercussions of Christina's visit, made her welcome and insisted that she should stay in the Palace in the rooms which had been her own when she was Queen.

There she was virtually a prisoner, for every possible means was devised to prevent her moving about the town.

Rumours were deliberately spread by Count Magnus that she would attempt to regain the throne, and, as a result a special meeting of the Diet was held on 19 October.

At this, to everyone's relief, Christina sent a memorandum requesting confirmation of the Abdication Act, and meekly asking that her claims for her overdue pension should be discussed.

There were many members of the Diet who suggested that if the financial problem was solved, she could probably be persuaded to go away again, but the clergy ignored this side of the question and complained bitterly about her continued presence in the country.

One reason for their anger was that Christina had deliberately revived a great interest in her religion and had Mass celebrated every day in a room at the Palace which she had turned into a chapel.

The clergy got their way, and the Diet sent Christina a reply that by breaking her oath always to support the Lutheran religion, she had forfeited all rights and privileges arranged at her abdication.

However, because she was a Vasa they were willing to continue to pay her provided she ceased performing the rites of the Catholic faith.

As none of the Regency felt like taking this ultimatum to

Christina, it was agreed that Archbishop Lenaeus should have a personal interview with her. It was an unpleasant half-hour which ended in angry words:

'We know what the Pope is trying to do through you,' the Archbishop warned her. 'He wants to get at our souls.'

'You do not know the Pope, and I do,' Christina replied. 'He would not give four crowns for all the souls of your clergymen put together.'

The prelate left, and promptly held a secret meeting at which the next move to oust their unwelcome guest was approved.

Just before Christmas, workmen invaded Christina's chapel and began to pull it down. She entered while they were at work, and there was an embarrassing moment when she pummelled and punched at the men in an attempt to stop them.

The same day her priests and some of her courtiers were taken in guarded coaches to Gothenberg and banished from Sweden.

On Christmas morning Christina managed to make up a small procession and she rode on a sled through the snow-covered streets to the private house of the French Ambassador where she attended Mass.

This defiant gesture infuriated the people of Stockholm, and she at last deemed it wiser to leave the city.

As she was most anxious to hear what her imposter had been doing at Nörkoping, she went there in the New Year, where she was for a time half forgotten.

As the days passed without any news, she wrote a rather ridiculous letter to the Estates declaring that if anything happened to the young King, the succession would have to revert to her, and if she declined the Crown, then it was her choice which would decide the identity of the new monarch.

Immediately the Estates sent her an ultimatum that if she did not sign another Act of Abdication renouncing for all time her claim to the Crown, she could not expect her income to continue.

Christina signed this document without any more complaints about the hostility which was shown to her, she let it be known that if they would give her some money she would leave the country for good.

The Estates managed to collect together a little more than 100,000 crowns, which was about half the sum that was due to her.

Possibly for the first time in Christina's life she realized she was beaten, and she set sail from Helsinborg in the middle of May for Hamburg.

Her financial affairs were again in such a hopeless muddle that she remained there for nearly a year, arguing and planning with Texeira, to discover some way of ensuring her future revenues, and solving the problem of the enormous debts that she had piled up.

Texeira had been very patient, but very few of the loans he had made to Christina had been repaid.

Eventually he arranged to give her an income of 100,000 crowns a year in return for which she would surrender all her rights to her revenues from Sweden.

It was estimated that if she could keep to what was to her a very modest income, and obey Azzolini's rules, her household debts would be gradually repaid.

All the time that she was in Hamburg Christina felt desperately lonely without Azzolini.

Hardly a week passed without her sending him a long adoring letter, to which he seldom troubled to reply. But he sent regular sums of money to the three members of the Queen's retinue who were in his confidence.

They were told to keep him informed of her every activity.

In April, 1661 Christina could bear to be away from him no longer, and she set out for Rome. Azzolini met her shortly after she had crossed the Alps and escorted her on the hot and dusty journey to the Eternal City.

Her appearance as she went straight to the Vatican was even stranger than her first visit.

She was dirty and dishevelled from the long journey, and only some Cardinal's stricture on etiquette prevented her from approaching the Pope in the dress of a man.

She adroitly overcame this difficulty by wearing a skirt of filmy lace through which her stained and muddy riding breeches could plainly be seen.

The Pope, who had been informed of her gesture to the Catholic religion in Sweden, ignored her costume and made her welcome.

At the sight of her all the doubts Azzolini had been experiencing as to the reality of his passion evaporated.

Her deep husky voice captivated and enthralled him as it

had done before, while Christina, in an ecstasy of happiness at being with him, was also at peace within herself.

For some months, at least, she was ready to watch the world go by. She wanted to play no leading role.

To be alone with her beloved Cardinal was all her hungry emotions asked of life and – love.

CHAPTER THIRTEEN

WHATEVER the real relationship of Christina and Dezio Azzolini may have been – and it intrigued contemporary Rome as strongly as it has interested posterity – both were utterly content in their being together after so long a separation.

Christina was naturally mischievous enough to tell all and sundry that she loved the Cardinal, but she also used the term to describe her regard for people she merely liked, so those who listened to her were often privately confused and doubtful as to the truth.

But her admiration of Azzolini was genuine, and excelled anything she felt for any other living person.

'He is the only man I know who is above flattery and a stranger to envy,' she once told the Pope, and the wise and tolerant old man nodded contentedly.

If his favourite children had to be slaves to the lusts of the flesh it were better that their desires should be raised above the level of a common intrigue by lofty feelings of virtue.

He was not perhaps so pleased with another paean of praise which Christina sang about her mentor and friend.

'Dezio has the mind and cleverness of a devil,' she exclaimed, 'the virtue of an angel, and the great and noble heart of an Alexander.'

Every facet of her behaviour showed that she was deeply in love with the handsome Cardinal, only three years older than herself. And Azzolini was as ambitious as his statesmanlike qualities amply justified.

Unlike all the other men Christina had fascinated and found fascinating, he had never coarsened his character by the more repellent amusements in which men of his age and social status habitually indulged.

The strumpets of Rome had gibed at him in his youth as being cold and effeminate. It was quite untrue. He was in fact very masculine and very virile.

Early in his adult life he had dispassionately examined the different paths of life.

Then he had deliberately chosen a fundamentally ascetic one because he believed that the rewards of the career in the Church which was open to him were infinitely more satisfying than the ephemeral delights of dalliance and gallantry.

Christina was the first woman to assail the fortress of his heart and mind.

But he realized in the brief period before her departure for France, when he had become a visitor in that reprehensible household in the Farnese Palace, that he had been within an ace of losing everything that he valued.

Only the patience of the Pope and the memory of his past services to the Vatican saved him.

Azzolini knew also that his appointment to Christina's household was the final trial of his character. His purely intimate life was his own affair, but his outward behaviour was under the close surveillance of his master and indeed of all Rome.

To serve Christina had, in the past, been to descend to the level of the mountebanks and rogues who battened on her generosity and had a contemptuous disregard for convention.

Few had been of worthy character when they entered her service, the majority emerged the worse for the experience.

Azzolini had to be the exception to the rule. He had no intention of failing the Pope who was gambling so heavily on his probity; besides, he felt a great pity for the talented and misunderstood Queen.

Inexorably he found the selfless emotion of his desire to help her changing as he came to know her better. Whatever succour Christina needed, it was certainly not pity.

When Azzolini accepted the truth of this, he was already in love with her.

Christina on her part felt utterly secure in her love. The enslavement of marriage which she had always dreaded was not a danger in the case of a priest. She knew, too, that Azzolini's regard for virtue was a byword, and she therefore had no jealous qualms.

Mentally he was her equal, and she never had that feeling for contempt for her lover which had marred so many of her previous infatuations.

It was not unnatural that, released from the repressions

engendered by her consuming jealousy and distaste of wifely enslavement, her natural femininity came to the surface and began to rule her life.

For the first time she experienced the contentment of turning to a man for advice, the happiness of explaining her problems and forebodings, and the joy of basking in the serenity of a wise protective security.

Apart from the mystery of their sexual attitude and activity, these two middle-aged people lived their daily lives like an established couple in whom the fiery passions of love had been disciplined by familiarity.

Christina would sit patiently on a chair beside Azzolini's desk as he explained the details of the household accounts.

With unaccustomed meekness she would agree to his suggestions for dismissal and engagement of servants until almost all her retinue consisted of reasonably honest and reliable persons.

There were Swiss soldiers in her bodyguard. Italians whose characters were well known to the Vatican took over the positions where money had to be handled and goods ordered.

The Cardinal even prevailed on her to employ women as tiring maids, although she could not bring herself to give them much to do.

There were, of course, occasions when the old emotional fires broke out, and she stormed and raved at the futility of her uneventful life.

Azzolini would let the outburst expend itself and then quietly put forward a cogent argument proving the foolish futility of her attitude.

A particularly difficult time occurred when Christina saw a chance of scoring a point against France, for that country's ostracism after the Monaldeschi incident still rankled.

Louis XIV sent a new ambassador to Rome. He was the Duc de Créqui, a man of extreme hauteur and of unpredictable temper.

Even before he arrived Christina made up her mind to dislike him if only because he was to live in the Farnese Palace, while the Duc sent an envoy ahead of him with instructions to ensure that 'the depredations of the Swedish ex-Queen and her mob of vandals' were rectified before he took possession.

Diplomatic etiquette demanded that a new Ambassador in Rome should include Christina in his introductory calls.

On such matters the Queen still adamantly refused to take Azzolini's advice, which almost always reflected an attitude of compromise.

She sent a peremptory reply deigning to see the French Ambassador but stressing that he could expect no more than a stool to sit on during the audience.

The Duc de Créqui was very conscious of his exalted birth and of the high office he held in the comity of nations. He replied that he required a chair as enjoyed by his equivalent in rank – a Cardinal of the Vatican.

The messenger who brought this ultimatum returned with another – 'there could be no audience.'

Azzolini saw that for once Christina's impetuosity was not without its advantages. He had been in audience with the Pope while the Queen was exchanging these messages and the conversation had been entirely about the new French Ambassador.

The Duc had sent impossible demands, the principal one being that diplomatic immunity should extend to anyone in Rome to whom he cared to give a note of authorization; also that the entire area around the Farnese Palace, where ostlers, tradesmen and the families and relatives of the Embassy servants lived, should be privileged ground.

The Pope was anxious that the newly organized diplomatic arrangements between France and the Papal States should develop smoothly, but a friendly atmosphere was not nearly so vital to Rome as to Versailles.

He told Azzolini that he felt positive the didactic attitude of the Duc was personal, and not official.

Christina's quarrel provided an excellent test of this theory.

At the Cardinal's request Christina wrote a mild and conciliatory letter to Louis XIV, stressing how disappointed she had been that his Ambassador had not seen fit to accept her hospitality on the only basis her position allowed.

Because of this, she added, she was writing to stress her loyalty to His Majesty – her only possible means of doing so as she could not voice such sentiments to his official representative of France.

Louis expressed his regrets and added that he had issued instructions which should banish such a regrettable incident from her mind.

The Duc de Créqui arrived at Christina's house a few days

later and glowered at her – sitting on a stool. He had obeyed without delay because even he began to realize that his dictatorial demands were creating serious trouble.

Christina's tenancy of the Farnese Palace had brought scandal enough, but the Duc's regime was already causing more.

As one man, the rogues and ruffians of Rome had found lodgings in the area which was technically French territory and therefore a sanctuary for them. They used it as a base for nocturnal hold-ups, burglaries and abductions.

The Pope could do nothing but reinforce the Papal police, who were tough and fearless as most of them had a lineage of brigands from Corsica behind them. His Holiness ordered them to throw a cordon round the Farnese Palace area.

The Duc moved to and fro while virtually besieged in his Embassy.

Soon after he had paid his respects to Christina, he issued another challenge to the Vatican. He refused to visit Cardinal Don Mario Chigi, the Pope's nephew, for no particular reason but that in his opinion the Cardinal was a private person and he talked to private persons only if he liked them.

Don Mario had some responsibility for the policing of Rome and he lost no time in letting the rank and file of the force know of the Ambassador's insult.

The Corsicans, who had been getting more and more incensed at the criminals who jeered at them from the security of diplomatic sanctuary, took the hint.

Brawls became frequent, and on 20 August, 1662, under the impression that a wanted man was returning to safety among a crowd of the Ambassador's personal attendants, they began a three-hours' siege of the Palace.

The moment anyone appeared at a window a fusillade of musket shot drove him back. The Duc himself narrowly escaped injury.

In the midst of it all a closed carriage approached, and the Corsicans fired into it. The occupant was the Ambassador's wife returning from Mass. She was dragged from the carriage. Her small page was killed.

The crisis was grave, and Azzolini had to leave Christina's house for prolonged conferences at the Vatican. Without his restraining hand she lunged into the fray, sending letters to everybody concerned.

To Azzolini himself she sent a characteristic suggestion that a Corsican policeman should be executed to avenge the death of the page-boy.

'If the culprit is not identified, then the innocent must suffer,' she wrote.

This and all her other suggestions were, of course, useless. The Duc de Créqui was withdrawn from Rome, and the Papal Nuncio was expelled from France.

French troops were deployed in readiness to take over the Palace of the Popes at Avignon, while a large force moved south preparatory for an invasion of the Papal States if the situation deteriorated.

Christina tasted the dregs of failure once again. The Pope voiced his exasperation at her interference in an extremely delicate situation; Louis indicated that even the formalities of his friendship with her were over.

The ultimate solution was a complete capitulation by the Pope, including the abolition of the Corsican Guard, the erection of a monument commemorating the attack, and the personal apology by Cardinal Don Mario Chigi to the King of France.

Despite the fact that Christina told everyone that 'the Pope will realize that I have done an important service in this affair' her sentiments were not echoed by His Holiness nor even by Azzolini.

For the first and only time a coolness sprang up between her and the Cardinal.

He was, perhaps, a little to blame for saying 'I told you so' when Christina wanted to know why the number of invitations to attend entertainments was noticeably decreasing, and why the complete loss of her friendship with France had not been replaced by a corresponding improvement in her relations with the Vatican.

Azzolini remained patient and loyal.

He had envisaged occasional problems of the kind when he shouldered the burden of being the Queen's counsellor as well as her friend.

He knew that a hundred scars from the perfidy of those around her had left her sensitive to any suspicion of divided or dying loyalties.

He showed his unswerving devotion by the quiet and efficient manner in which he continued to run her household, and by a thousand charming little gestures of practical flattery for her comfort and well-being.

These included comfits for her horses which were magnificently stabled and had become one of her passions at the time, and rare plants that he personally brought and planted in her garden.

The Queen always pretended to feel contempt for any woman who glowed with pleasure at little gestures of this kind, insisting that they were typical of the cunning of men who enslaved by symbolic but easily contrived tokens of adoration.

Azzolini, however, knew only too well that she protested too much, and that in reality she longed for them.

At times – momentarily, but not more than momentarily – Christina would admit to herself the fundamental contradiction of her character, and that she was indeed her worst and only enemy.

The months ticked away. Christina realized that on her next birthday she would be forty, and so little of what she had dreamed had been accomplished. She looked back on her life since she had come to the Riario Palace.

What she saw appalled her.

She was subsiding into the lethargic routine of late middle age, being drugged by the steady monotony of a household run smoothly but with a dreary correctitude under Azzolini's careful accounting.

As she examined her position she told herself that the banal aura of uneventful respectability was engendered simply because of her lack of money.

Texeira was still doing his best, but less than half of the pension due to her was being paid to him by Sweden, and even that was two years in arrears.

She managed to persuade Azzolini to allow her to send delegates to Stockholm to inquire about the position. They went, reliable and sensible men, equipped with cogent arguments of the Cardinal's devising.

He was just and fair, and he expected his reasoned statement of affairs to be studied, accepted and acted upon with justice. Argument, however, was not the weapon to use in a skirmish with the Swedish Regency.

Utterly unscrupulous and venal, the only thing its members could have understood was intimidation.

When a kinsman of Azzolini's, an honest young man named

Lorenzo Adami, returned and reported to Christina that some of her money had been loaned to a distinguished member of the Government, she asked his identity. The answer merely confirmed her suspicions.

'The money was demanded by the Swedish Chancellor, Count Magnus de la Gardie,' Adami replied.

It was enough for Christina. Her hatred for the man she had once loved drove her to plan a quick revenge. She made plans for a second visit to Sweden.

In May, 1666, she set off, with a small suite of sixteen people, among whom, at Azzolini's insistence, was a lady-in-waiting named Françoise Landini, a lovely Frenchwoman of great charm and few morals.

Christina rode on horseback and she went so fast, often insisting on riding through the night, that some of her entourage fell out.

Through sheer exhaustion she had to pause a while at Trent where her old ebullience caused her to throw discretion to the winds.

She stayed at a small inn where the only bed was some straw on the floor. Early next morning a stranger asked to see her.

When he entered he bowed low and then knelt at her feet, adoration and a profound respect in his eyes. Christina was delighted, for deep obeisance was something she greatly missed.

She studied him carefully before she gave permission for him to speak. He was one of those men who are so ugly that they exert an incredible fascination on women.

His physique was magnificent – a lean and iron-hard body, long legs and narrow thighs. His face had a deceptive appearance of great suffering, with its hollow eyes, and lantern jaw.

In striking contrast to his swarthy complexion his hair was blonde, almost colourless.

'I am Horatio de Bourbon, Marquis del Monte, Your Majesty,' he began – and his voice was deep and melodious. 'You have perhaps heard of me?'

Christina had certainly heard of him. The Marquis del Monte had been banished from the Papal States and was a personal enemy of the Pope's nephew, Don Mario Chigi.

The Queen saw a perfect opportunity for repaying the slights she had endured from the latter during the de Créqui affair.

'I am told that your Marquisate is very poor,' she began.

'It is a poor place, Your Majesty,' del Monte agreed. 'The Apennines do not permit a prosperous peasantry nor are they a centre of trade. But my family has not been without resources in providing the means of livelihood – at least until jealousies in some quarters of which you know made it necessary for me to put the Alps between my persecutors and myself.'

The humble deference was gone. The Marquis grinned insolently and looked at Christina with the challenging eyes that had enabled him to create a reputation of being one of the most lascivious and irresistible men in Italy.

Christina grinned back. She knew that his family's means of livelihood had been to turn the Marquisate into a robbers' nest.

The whole area swarmed with bandits, who preyed on travellers and pack trains in all the bordering states and then sheltered from justice in the protecting arms of the del Monte family.

It was a large and remarkable unit, the male members of it having a tradition that whatever fate held in store for the unfortunate women they abducted the bastard children which resulted should gain all the dubious benefits of wearing the del Monte crest.

Their right to this being as unconventional as their insistence that their line shared – albeit with a bar sinister – the illustrious ancestry of Charlemagne.

Before the interview ended Christina was completely under del Monte's dominance. She offered him a place in her suite, whereupon he warned her that:

'Everything I can lay my hands on, whether sacred or profane, is my own.'

She was delighted with his bravado, and felt that the with-held moneys from Sweden were as good as in her hands. The Marquis was being more frank than she realized.

He robbed her from the first day that he was in her employment, taking the money from her for the innkeeper and then telling the wretched man that he would be paid by the Queen on her return.

The remainder of the journey to Hamburg was made at a more leisurely pace.

Christina's tardiness enabled a few of Azzolini's letters to arrive first at Texeira's house, and despite the complete ascendancy which the gallant Marquis had gained over her, she shut herself in her room while she read them.

Christina had written a number of letters to the Cardinal during the journey, carefully avoiding any details of del Monte's activities, but contenting herself with the brief announcement that he had joined her suite.

These letters were, of course, still in transit to Rome, but when they arrived they caused Azzolini profound misgivings.

Perhaps he suspected worse than was in fact the case.

For the Marquis had a taste for more youthful charmers than Christina, and apart from his affairs with the ladies of the town, he had begun to lay siege to the affections of Françoise Landini, the Queen's lady-in-waiting, whose husband had been left behind in Rome.

Christina, not unnaturally, quickly recovered from the infatuation she had at first felt for del Monte.

But she found a certain vicarious pleasure in having him recount the stories of his conquests when he came to see her each morning for the ostensible purpose of discussing the household accounts.

She had appointed him Master of the Household, a position almost precisely the same as the Cardinal still held in Rome, but with devastatingly different results.

The boring details of food bills and servants' wages were forgotten while this swashbuckling Lothario boasted of his exploits.

'You seem to think you have absolute authority to seduce every woman you meet,' she said archly.

'I believe I have,' the Marquis retorted.

It was not long before irate husbands and vengeful fathers were demanding audience with the Queen to protest about the Master of her Household.

They were at first delighted by her sympathy when she insisted on hearing every detail of their complaints but then were infuriated when at the story's end she roared with laughter.

Del Monte's amorous adventures cost money, and as he was desperately in need of funds he conceived the ingenious idea of holding to ransom Texeira's favourite nephew, a handsome young Jew named Abraham.

To make certain that he would ride in the forests around

Brunswick the Marquis purchased a fine white horse on the Queen's credit and presented it to the young man.

When Abraham's disappearance was reported del Monte immediately offered to arrange a search party if the Jewish financier would pay for the expenses incurred.

To this the anxious man instantly agreed, and after several days the Marquis returned to say that he had located some soldier deserters who had abducted his nephew and demanded thirty thousand rix dollars as a ransom.

Eventually Texeira handed over ten thousand dollars to del Monte and his nephew was returned.

In fairness to Christina, it must be said that she had no idea whatsoever of this diabolical scheme. Her own reaction was intense admiration for the bravery and resourcefulness of the Marquis in bringing the abduction to such a happy conclusion.

She spent most of her days in writing letters and pondering on her best method of attaining her objectives in Sweden.

Once a week a horseman went to Rome with letters for Azzolini. They were full of nostalgic affection. Parts of them were in a simple code in which such phrases as 'tenderest emotion' and 'till death do us part' were mixed with initial letters conveying more intimate sentiments.

The Cardinal's replies were more practical, but his declarations of reciprocated love became less frequent as he obtained news of Christina's activities in Hamburg from those servants he had paid to keep him informed.

When a letter arrived from him which charged the Queen with a return to her old extravagances, and particularizing them while contrasting his own problems in keeping even a skeleton staff at her Rome house, she flew into a violent temper.

Imperiously she summoned the man she thought was an informer, a mild little physician Azzolini had sent along to look after her health. Before the doctor had a chance to defend himself Christina grabbed him by the throat and began to throttle him.

Del Monte, who knew from his own sources of information that she had got hold of the wrong man, rescued the gasping doctor just in time.

The Marquis had been reading all Azzolini's letters for some time, having persuaded his infatuated mistress Françoise to steal them from Christina's room while she slept and replace them in the morning.

He gauged from the unfortunate details which were known to the Cardinal the identity of those who were informing on the Queen, and he either had them dismissed or offered them a larger bribe to keep quiet.

Meantime the news from Sweden was depressing. Christina heard reliably but unofficially that Count Magnus had hurriedly appointed a secret commission which had rushed through resolutions designed to refuse her admission to Sweden.

She was to enter the country only when the Estates were in session, who could thus deal instantly with any political crisis her presence created; she was not to practise her religion either privately or publicly; and she was to bring no officer of the Catholic Church with her.

Having passed these resolutions in secret, the Council of State thereupon allowed them to leak out so that Christina would hear of them.

She dared not risk the degradation of being turned back at the coast, and for that reason she had to acquiesce as regards the first condition.

As Count Magnus delayed the meeting of the Estates time after time he effectively wore down her patience. But not as much as he hoped, for instead of becoming exasperated and returning to Rome she remained at Hamburg, realizing that sometime the government of the country would have to meet.

All through the closing months of 1666 she hung on, desperately impoverished and in growing anger.

It was another of the bitterly cold winters of that century. She was ill and tired and became ready to compromise instead of challenge.

Her next letter to the Regency Council in Stockholm was almost meek in its tone. She listed the people she wished to bring with her, including the name of her secretary, Santini.

The Council was, of course, quite unaware of this man's calling. He was in fact a priest from Tuscany with an extremely poor reputation at the Vatican.

Cardinal Azzolini had strongly advised Christina against his engagement, offering instead two prudent and godly men approved by the Pope.

This official commendation had been sufficient to confirm

Christina's objections to them, and the Abbot Santini had been instantly engaged.

His unworthiness soon showed itself.

He became the close friend of del Monte, and there were many scandalous stories about him which confirmed to the good people of Hamburg all that they suspected about the Catholic religion in general and Christina's *ménage* in particular.

By the end of February everything was ready for the journey. The weather was, however, impossible, deep snow-drifts and hard frosts alternating with sudden thaws and floods. Not until 28 April was Christina able to start. The King of Denmark provided a ship to take her across the Sound to Helsinborg.

There, because the Swedish Government was anxious at all costs to avoid fomenting civil disturbances by insulting a member of the nation's beloved Vasa dynasty, representatives awaited her in state.

In order to ensure a reliable report on Christina, Count Magnus had sent his young nephew, Count Pontus de la Gardie, to greet her.

To her delight and amazement she was escorted through lines of saluting soldiers to the best house in the town where everything to the last detail for her comfort had been prepared

Always hungry for gestures of affection and never able to believe ill of anyone for long, Christina's spirits rose as she walked through the beautifully furnished rooms. She was unable to see the cunning hand of Count Magnus behind every ostentatious gesture of hospitality.

The uncouth attitude of the Government on the Queen's previous visit had annoyed the people of Sweden; they had begun to wonder who was the sinner and who was the more sinned against.

This time the Count hoped to force all blame for the troubles he expected on to Christina's shoulders.

The journey to Stockholm took a week. The people turned out to see her for reasons of curiosity. They remained to stare at her in admiration.

The haughty sneering sovereign who had defied them in years gone by had gone; in her stead was a plump, gay little woman who looked at the hills and lakes of her native land with obvious longing.

Moreover age had accentuated the Vasa characteristics. There was no doubt that Christina was the daughter of the heroic Gustavus Adolphus. She held herself erect and sat her horse well.

She rode fearlessly ahead of the mounted pikemen and laughed with pleasure as the crowd pressed forward. She had courage, this storm bird who struck fear into the hearts of the loathsome dictators of the Regency Council.

She was of different stuff from the puny little boy King who had been spirited away to Uppsala in case his aunt's very presence in the capital should contaminate him.

Then, through her foolishness in bringing Santini along, all the goodwill was dissipated by a tawdry little incident.

While Christina was resting at Nyköping, awaiting permission to proceed to Stockholm, a girl came from a neighbouring village to see the Queen of whom her parents talked so much.

Santini was enraptured with her Nordic beauty and forced his attentions on her. She repulsed him, but he followed her through the streets and assaulted her.

Only her screams, which brought a crowd of people hurrying to her, saved her from being raped.

Santini fled to the safety of Christina's house, but when the journey was resumed the girl's father hurled himself at the carriage conveying Santini and del Monte.

A crowd of people, realizing what was happening, joined in the attack. Santini had to seek refuge in Christina's coach, which fortunately she was using as the day was wet, and she ordered the guards to close round and protect her so-called secretary.

In the excitement she used the expression 'man of God' and her secret was out.

The news that the Queen had brought a priest with her was rushed to Stockholm, and back came the Regency's ultimatum.

She must expel Santini from the country and give her promise not to celebrate Mass in her own household or at the French Embassy. Otherwise 'measures for the security of the official religion of the State would be put in hand'.

Count Magnus, who was, of course, the fount of this insulting note, was in effect threatening deportation.

The inevitability of defeat produced a certain majesty of behaviour in the Queen. Count Magnus was undoubtedly expecting a silly show of defiance which he could have used to arouse the religious fervour of the people. But Christina's dignified attitude in public, however much she stormed in private, swung the nation to her side in sympathy.

As she returned to the coast, cutting out rest periods but never passing through towns and villages at a speed which would have suggested flight, the people turned out to cheer her.

If Pope Alexander VII had not died suddenly while Christina's magnificent gesture to her adopted religion was being made all Catholic Europe would have organized joyful celebrations in her honour.

Even though the Church was mourning, the account of the Swedish Queen's staunch attitude was told in all churches.

Dearest to her of all the eulogies which awaited her when she reached Hamburg once more was an affectionate letter from Azzolini.

He told her of his pleasure and admiration in terms more enthusiastically worded than she had ever known from him.

A month later Christina heard with relief that an old friend of Azzolini and hers, Cardinal Giulio Rospigliosi, had been elected Pope. She had been very worried about the identity of the new Vicar of Christ because a number of the likely candidates heartily disliked her.

Among them was Cardinal Farnese who nursed the bitter experience of Christina as a tenant in his house, and later complaints about her had been almost daily on his desk while he was Civil Governor of Rome.

The new Pope, named Clement IX, was an unworldly man who either ignored the gossip about the Queen or forgave her misdemeanours because he genuinely admired her intellectual prowess and her interest in the arts.

Christina decided that the accession of the new Pope gave her a glorious chance to create some excitement, for life was extremely dull in Hamburg, and nobody in the Protestant town was really taking any notice of her.

She knew full well that the city had been unusually tolerant in allowing her to remain there for such a long time, and to have the freedom of practising her religion.

She confined her devotions to quiet celebrations of the Mass behind closed doors, but with the news of the accession of the new Pope she immediately launched into plans to make her rejoicings as ostentatious and noisy as she could possibly conceive.

The civic authorities, who had the duty of punishing the practice of the Catholic faith by its citizens with long terms of imprisonment, watched with profound misgivings the signs of activity which began outside Christina's house.

This was in the main street and had an imposing frontage with an open courtyard.

The Queen suddenly announced that Mass would be celebrated in the hall of the house, the front of which formed one side of the courtyard, while the Marquis del Monte offered to arrange the decorations which Christina wanted to cover the exterior walls.

He was not likely to miss a chance of making a handsome commission for himself whenever Christina could be persuaded to spend some money.

On this occasion she had very little, but the persuasive Marquis arranged for her to have extended credit with numerous tradesmen, although, of course, his own commission on the contracts he made on her behalf had to be paid strictly in cash.

The Mass was held at mid-morning on 25 July, 1667, and Christina caused several cannon to be fired during the elevation of the Host.

This naturally had the desired effect of drawing great crowds to the vicinity of the house.

Then draperies which had concealed the decorations on the buildings were drawn aside and the people saw some highly coloured ornamentations which displayed the arms of the new Pope.

There were angels flying through clouds above it, and a symbolic figure representing the Church of Rome trampling on heretics. The latter, who writhed in agony below, were portrayed as extremely ugly people, most of them with profound German characteristics.

For the rest of that day the crowds shuffled about staring at the decorative effect and grumbling in low voices that the eccentric woman who was the guest of their city should be allowed to break the law in this way.

When the grumbling began to grow louder, Christina adroitly staved off the inevitable trouble by unveiling a fountain which had been built at the front of the courtyard right on the edge of the street, from which wine spouted through nine different holes.

At the sight of this the mob surged forward catching the liquid in their hats, some falling into the basin in their efforts to drink the pool of wine at the base.

The news of this lavish hospitality spread like wildfire. Soon crowds were arriving with beakers and basins and any kind of receptacle with which to drink the health of Christina, the new Pope and anyone else that her lackeys moving among them suggested.

When at last the supplies of wine which del Monte had managed to obtain on credit ran out, it was already twilight and this was the cue for Christina's *pièce de résistance.*

Servants leaned out of windows and set fire to the illuminations which surrounded the set-piece. At the same time the cannon fired salutes and the crowd momentarily fell back in fear.

The shock of the noise did not sober them, for everyone there was by this time far too drunk, but it did result in their jollification abruptly turning to anger.

The Protestant Church authorities had been horrified at what had been going on, and when it was seen that there was no chance of stopping the orgy, it did the next best thing.

Agents were sent into the mob to whisper that Christina had spent all this money simply to destroy the established religion of the country, and to allow treacherous Rome to regain the influence which in the past it had taken so many lives to destroy.

Christina had watched the scene from an upper window and in her usual way of utterly failing to appreciate that anybody could misconstrue her designs, she imagined that the howls and shouting below were applause.

Her bedroom overlooked the courtyard, and, tired from the excitement of the day, she prepared for bed.

Just as she was half-undressed, a shower of stones smashed the windows. She hastily extinguished her candles and looked out.

The light from the torches round the decorations illuminated her face and another fusillade of brickbats was hurled at her.

She backed away quickly and screamed orders to her servants to extinguish the lights and drive the people from the courtyard.

She put any weapon she could find into their hands, and they did make some attempt to obey, but by this time the mob was hammering at the door and amidst all the clamour could be heard a repeated monotone:

'Kill her, kill her, kill her.'

Del Monte, who was really alarmed at the way things were going, gave orders to half a dozen men to prime their muskets and fire a round of shot.

They obeyed him more exactly than he had intended, aiming straight into the crowd instead of over their heads.

Several men and women fell dead, and more were wounded. This roused the mob to a state of mania which brooked no resistance. Christina escaped by a back door to the house of the Swedish Minister, where she claimed diplomatic sanctuary.

In the meantime, the municipal authorities, fearing that the town would be in a state of riot, sent troops to restore order.

Next morning, despite the protests of her host, the Queen insisted on walking through the streets to see the damage.

A crowd of several thousand people were standing outside her house, but they sullenly made way for her, and the presence of troops prevented any attack.

She immediately let it be known that she intended to pay compensation to the bereaved families, and would see that the wounded had medical attention.

Luckily for her the level-headed Hamburgers accepted the fact that she had not really intended to foment trouble and within three days the damage to her house was repaired.

Once again she settled into a quiet routine while the people of the city did their best to ignore her.

There was for the moment no reason for her to think up any new ideas to focus the glaring light of publicity on herself, because she had become tremendously interested in black magic. Her tutor in the Satanic arts was a heretic named Borri.

He was an Italian who escaped burning at the stake by fleeing to Germany, while the Church authorities made a gesture of punishment by burning an effigy of him in one of the largest squares in Rome.

The man was a remarkable personality who had certainly achieved some miraculous cures in many parts of Europe and there were many people who regarded him as a saint.

But it is uncertain as to whether he really believed that he could make gold or if he decided that the generous supplies of money which Christina gave him for his experiments permitted a more comfortable life than he had known since he was branded as a heretic.

Certainly the two of them spent hours together in one of the rooms of her house which she had turned into a small laboratory and an enormous amount of weird chemicals and valuable materials was wasted in their attempts to make gold.

Borri was more ambitious than most of the alchemists of his day.

He told Christina that the Philosopher's Stone was quite an important discovery, but he himself believed that he was on the track of a fluid which was even more powerful. It simply had to be poured over anything to infuse it with gold.

Christina was gullible enough to believe this rigmarole and she meekly obeyed his every command to her, working as his servant.

In the evenings she wrote long and enthusiastic letters to Azzolini in Rome, telling him of the day's work and saying how wonderful it would be when all her financial troubles were solved with this magic fluid.

The Cardinal did not worry overmuch at first, but when he gathered from her letters that she was becoming more and more enamoured of Borri personally, he decided that the matter had gone far enough.

He wrote and said that as a heretic the alchemist was extremely dangerous, and if Christina continued to employ him, he himself would have to reconsider his position:

'I cannot remain your friend and ally if you have this man in your employment,' he warned her.

That was enough.

That very morning, Christina went into the laboratory, swept the retorts and bottles of liquid on to the floor and told Borri that she never wanted to see him again.

He could do nothing but flee from her house, and he went to Denmark where for some time he persuaded King Frederick III to finance his experiments.

Shortly afterwards he was arrested by Catholic agents and imprisoned for life. It was rumoured that the enterprising Marquis del Monte received payment for his capture.

Once again Christina was lonely and left with nothing to do in a hostile and suspicious city.

CHAPTER FOURTEEN

WHILE Christina worried about her finances and regretted her placid behaviour during her abortive visit to Sweden, the Diet had been busily teaching Count Magnus de la Gardie and his friends in the Regency Council a lesson in manners.

The members voiced the worried conscience of the nation by insisting that their Queen must be treated with more honour and kindliness.

Despite the angry threats of Count Magnus they insisted that Christina be informed that past errors were to be atoned.

A courier was sent to Hamburg to inform her that all the financial terms of the Abdication Act would in future be observed, and that if she cared to visit her country again she and her suite would be given every facility to exercise their religious rites without hindrance.

Christina glowed with pleasure when she learned of the Diet's gesture of friendship.

Although the easing of her monetary problems was the most important practical benefit, her comment to Azzolini in the letter she wrote to him reporting the good news showed that she was most concerned with the Swedish nation's regard for her.

'The people love me,' she wrote. 'Only the ruling faction hate and fear me, and time will prove it.'

It was tempting to take the Diet at its word and return to Sweden in full state. She pondered on the repercussions which she felt sure she could cause.

A *coup d'état* which would put her on the throne of the Vasas was certainly not beyond all possibility and, failing this, she might in time foster a religious revolution so that the Northern lands returned in triumph to the true Church of Christ.

Yet in her heart she knew that these were only the dreams of a youthful mind in an ageing body. She was tired of gambling, and even the attractive prize of the Swedish throne did not really tempt her any more.

The restless spirit of urgency which had so long impelled her to challenge fortune had died. The enthusiasm and vitality which would have made her battle for her homeland had gone.

Instead she contented herself with waiting for Fate to offer her in its own good time smaller and more easily attainable prizes. Soon, she thought wistfully, she would be able to return to the security of Rome and to Azzolini.

Meantime there was every reason to celebrate her good fortune in having her credit restored. The surly Hamburg tradesmen could be put in their place now that they could be given a glimpse of the formally drawn-up resolution of the Swedish Diet.

She called in the Marquis del Monte and informed him that she wanted to give an entertainment.

He instantly appointed himself Superintendent of the Revels and got to work. Near Christina's house was a large vacant space used for the intricate game of Royal court tennis.

This the Marquis rented, and had tiers of seats erected around three sides of it with a stage at the end.

The time was September and a fine autumn period had set in. The Marquis decided on an open-air feast to follow the rather lascivious comedy a hack writer had plagiarized from the French.

He obtained a vast supply of candles and rushlights which he promised the Queen would outdo the sun itself. A ballet followed the gargantuan supper which lasted for four hours, and then came a fancy dress ball.

Christina appeared as a Queen of some unidentifiable Oriental kingdom, complete with a squadron of magnificent and half-naked slaves.

Del Monte had invited large numbers of the ladies of the town and by the early hours of the morning the whole affair had degenerated into debauchery.

Christina was the only person there who tasted no wines the whole evening, but she was as intoxicated as the rest. Not for years had she known such gaiety.

She enjoyed every second of it, but the next day she realized that such revels belonged to youth; she fell into a coma of exhaustion and had to be bled.

The Marquis del Monte suffered not one whit from it all.

He was up by mid-morning, calculating with great satisfaction the splendid profit he had made by defrauding the Queen on every item of the huge bill for the entertainment.

It was the Queen's farewell gesture to Hamburg.

A few days later, at the urgent insistence of Cardinal Azzolini, she set out for Rome. All along the route letters from him awaited her, demanding that she should hurry.

She was mystified and a little annoyed at his peremptory orders and she made no special effort to obey.

The Marquis del Monte encouraged her to tarry. He had considerable misgivings about the future.

Christina assured him that as a member of her staff he was beyond the reach of the Papal police and while he served her the outlaw edict was void.

He accepted this, but he had heard sufficient about the Cardinal holding precisely the same post as himself to wonder if his lucrative source of income would cease the moment the Royal procession reached Rome.

Christina arrived in Rome late in November, 1668.

Immediately Azzolini insisted on a long conference with her about the developments which had occurred in the past few weeks.

Christina's kinsman, John Casimir, had terminated his disastrous reign of Poland, during which he had brought defeat and disgrace on his kingdom by almost his every action. He had abdicated that September.

'There are four candidates for the throne,' the Cardinal explained. 'The most favoured at the moment is the Prince of Conde, whom Louis is backing to strengthen France's political influence in Eastern Europe. The Hapsburgs have nominated the Duke of Lorraine, and the Czar of Russia is offering his son.'

'The Poles must hate them all,' Christina exclaimed.

'Exactly,' the Cardinal replied. 'They hate the Austrians, the French and the Russians with equal intensity. That is why I have already put in motion an idea of my own. The Pope has agreed. A Nuncio is already in Warsaw with a secret letter to the Polish Diet in which the Pope advises adoption of my nominee. Do you know who that is?'

'Of course,' said Christina without surprise, 'I would make a good King of Poland. I hope you have stressed that I would never consent to the title of Queen.'

'They would agree to that,' the Cardinal answered. 'There is, however, another rather delicate point. My investigations show that their only objection is that you are unmarried. I have told them that this is not a problem without a possible solution.'

Christina hardly heard him. She was already envisaging the difficulties and the advantages of the Polish throne.

'I suppose not,' she said vaguely.

'No, of course not,' Azzolini insisted. 'But the matter of marriage is not of itself the important point. The real objection is that, in the opinion of the Polish Diet, the new reign would not be blessed with an heir.'

Christina was furious.

'They insult my womanhood, and cast aspersions on my age,' she said angrily. 'Are they suggesting that I am too old for bearing a child?'

'I have told them, in confidence of course, that I have reason to know that their fears are groundless,' Azzolini replied.

'And will continue to be so for the next ten years,' snapped the forty-two-year-old Christina.

Her sense of humour returned. She laughed merrily into the worried eyes of the man she had loved for so long.

Never in her life had she seen him so disturbed. She found it strange to have the tables turned; she to be with doubts and he wishing to throw discretion to the winds.

She saw clearly that he had come to the greatest crisis of his career and had made his decision. The call of the Church would give way to the glory of a throne. He was ready to be her Consort and the father of a Royal line.

She recognized the enormity of his choice, for Cardinal Azzolini's position was second in importance in the Papal States to the Pope himself, while everyone said with some justification that he would in the fullness of time ascend to the Chair of St. Peter.

The Queen felt at that moment a new and even deeper love for Dezio Azzolini.

Never before had she appreciated so fully the sensitive subtlety of his character, the fine clarity of his mind. If circumstances had favoured her she would undoubtedly have rejoiced in this belated marriage as much as in the acquisition of a crown.

But once again her dreams and aspirations dissolved into

thin air. The Poles decided their own destiny, choosing a native noble, Duke Wisnowieski, as their new monarch.

Christina found rather to her surprise that she was relieved at the unexpected turn of events.

'I shall be glad to die among human beings in Rome. If I had reigned and ended my life in Poland I would have been among beasts,' she told the Pope when she dined with him.

This was an unheard-of honour, for there was a tradition that no woman ate and drank at the same time as His Holiness.

The Pope replied that he appreciated the compliment, but he regretted the failure of his plans. To mark his disappointment, he handed Christina a document which promised her an annual pension of 12,000 crowns for as long as she lived.

The first payment was made immediately, and this unexpected addition to her resources enabled her to launch into an activity which had been occupying her mind for some time despite earlier failures.

She could not banish the feeling that the enormous wealth for which she craved was attainable by magic.

She was, of course, by no means unique in believing that the Philosopher's Stone was a scientific certainty, even if its discovery entailed methods objectionable to those who obeyed the strict letter of Catholic law.

Characteristically Christina determined to waste no time in getting to work. Workmen arrived to construct a laboratory, complete with furnaces and running water pumped from the near-by Tiber.

Assistants were easy to find. They besieged the palace as soon as the news of the building alterations got about.

The Queen was as usual defrauded right and left by charlatans who sold her equipment and ingredients which they insisted were vital for her experiments.

Cardinal Azzolini felt some misgivings about this new enthusiasm. But although the invocation of magic was obviously in contravention of the rules of the Church, he secretly wondered if there was anything in it.

Accordingly he took the middle course of attempting to control waste of money and, at the same time, furthering the experiments by appointing a chemist he knew personally.

Bandiere was the son of an apothecary in the little town of Romagnis near Bologna.

The Cardinal had a serious talk with him as soon as Christina approved his appointment, and made him personally responsible for keeping expenditure within reasonable bounds.

Bandiere obediently supplied meticulous accounts of his expenses every month, but they still mounted to as much as 4,000 livres.

There were unfortunately no successful results to report, and in fact the receipts made out by Bandiere were often for non-existent commodities.

However, Christina liked the alchemist very much, for he was wise enough to treat her with great veneration and to pretend to be enormously impressed with her knowledge of chemistry.

When, however, the experiments continued to end in failure the Queen's temper became more unpredictable and there were times when she chased the unfortunate man all round the laboratory, hurling any missile at him that came to her hand.

After a few experiences of this kind, Bandiere took the precaution of concealing a pistol inside his clothes in case the quarrel became too serious.

Christina worked in the laboratory for some time every day and, towards the end of the first year of work, she put Bandiere on a regular fee basis, with the object of making him a permanent servant in her home.

He was extremely well off under this arrangement, for he was given sufficient money to buy all the materials that he alleged were needed, and he soon became a hopeless drunkard.

Only Christina's enthusiasm for chemistry saved him from the complete destruction of his health, because his evening amusements were often spoiled when she insisted on working with him until the early hours of the morning, his only job being to stoke the furnaces ceaselessly for six or seven hours at a time.

When a large instalment of money came to the Queen from Sweden, she almost forgot her plans for the manufacture of gold. But the resourceful Bandiere saw to it that his usefulness in her household was not questioned.

He took up archaeology and wandered around Rome and its countryside digging up graves and bringing any trinkets he found to Christina.

Often she rewarded him with delight but just as often boxed him on the ears because the relic did not please her. Soon, however, the windfall from Sweden ran out and once again she resumed her experiments.

Azzolini was greatly upset by Bandiere's influence. He was jealous of Christina's admiration for the alchemist and worried about his fraudulent practices, not on account of their continued failure but because of the expense.

Facing the fact that it was quite impossible to persuade Christina to dismiss Bandiere until he was proved beyond all doubts to be a rogue, the Cardinal met deceit with cunning.

'There is much poverty in Rome this winter,' he told Christina one day. 'I think it would be a good gesture if you would distribute alms each month until the spring. Bandiere can find the deserving cases.'

Christina agreed to the proposal and Bandiere was sent out that evening with a purse containing a hundred crowns. Perhaps the Queen was already suspecting him, for she ordered him to bring certificates of dire need from the local priests.

Bandiere went to his room and forged a few certificates. The rest of the night and for the remainder of the month he distributed his charity among the inmates of Rome's bawdy houses.

When these activities lessened in their appeal he went around genuinely poor homes and offered charity in return for the virtue of the wife or daughter of the household.

Any woman who indignantly refused was reported to Christina as a person of scandalous behaviour and an unfit recipient for her charity.

It was not long before local priests and the insulted women themselves were reproaching Cardinal Azzolini, as the Queen's representative, to complain about Bandiere's behaviour.

He told them that the matter was out of his hands and he advised them to insist on reporting direct to the Queen.

Christina refused to believe their accusations and the scandal became so great that the Pope wrote her a personal letter advising her to get rid of Bandiere immediately.

The alchemist heard about it, and immediately rushed to Christina and begged her to protect him. She was considerably annoyed to hear of any interference with her affairs and she told him not to worry.

'These wicked priests would ruin you with me,' she told him. 'Laugh at them all for I will always take care of you.'

She was as good as her word, and for a time Bandiere lived in her house so that there was no chance of the Papal guard capturing him. He on his part continued to find new interests for the Queen.

He let it be known that he was on the track of the Universal Medicine, which was a fluid which could guarantee that anyone who drank it would live for one hundred years.

Christina was delighted at the news and assured Bandiere that she would take the concoction the moment it was ready.

This alarmed the alchemist and when Christina became more and more impatient because he could not produce results, he was panic-stricken and mixed various ingredients into a noisome fluid which he said he believed was the Universal Medicine at last.

He had taken the precaution of adding flavours and an aroma which he considered made it virtually impossible for anyone to swallow it.

This, however, did not worry Christina and she drank several spoonsful. Next morning she was seriously ill, her abdomen swelling so much that her valet rushed about the house saying that his mistress was about to burst asunder.

The swelling subsided during the day and Christina seemed to have borne no grudge against Bandiere, blaming her own body for its failure to absorb the poisonous fluid she had taken.

She was, however, less enthusiastic about the Universal Medicine after another magician, who was English by birth, managed to gain audience with her.

He assured her that he had the real secret remedy for prolonging life and gave her various circumstantial accounts of people he had treated in England and France who, although they were fifty or sixty years of age, behaved like persons thirty years younger.

He added that he was quite certain that they would remain in perfect health and vigour until they were one hundred and twenty or more.

He was in fact quite a young man, but swore to Christina that he was seventy years of age.

Seeing that even the gullible Queen was doubting some of his claims, he resourcefully produced a number of forged testimonials from people of quality who said that not only had they been cured of various diseases but had been made extremely youthful.

Finally he played his trump card.

'You know, Your Majesty, that the Marquis del Monte is sixty years of age, and you know also how vigorous and virile he is. I assure you that the reason is that he has permitted me to carry out my experiments on him.'

There was no more to be said. Christina was agog to try the remedy which had seemingly proved so successful with the Marquis.

She begged the Englishman to state his price for the recipe, but he refused to sell it, saying that he would furnish her with sufficient of the liquid to prove his claims, but without giving her enough for other people.

'Everyone has told me that you are the most generous Queen in the world,' he said ingratiatingly. 'If I gave you a large quantity, or the recipe for it, I know that you would supply it to many people and my source of livelihood would be gone.'

Christina became all the more eager to have this wonderful knowledge. She offered him 10,000 crowns for the secret, upon condition that he should leave Italy immediately.

The alchemist refused and at every meeting after that the price offered to him went higher and higher, principally because the Marquis del Monte was secretly meeting him in the evening and encouraging him to raise the figure.

The Marquis was quite positive Christina would never admit defeat and he was to receive a handsome commission on the transaction.

To make certain of this, del Monte would go to Christina and give intimate details of the benefits he himself had felt from the remedy, and urge her not to let the secret escape.

When the offer reached 30,000 crowns Azzolini heard about it and began to wonder how on earth he could stop this nonsense for good. He told Christina that he could not understand how an intelligent woman could possibly believe such rubbish.

The Queen was furious at his insinuation that she was being defrauded.

'My secret when I have bought it will be vehemently desired by some people and cause others to rejoice,' she said. 'I hope in God to live long enough to see a dozen more Popes and maybe a dozen more Cardinals in my household.'

Azzolini reminded Christina that every doctor in Rome was

worried about her mode of living, with her irregular meals and over-exertion both of her mind and body.

'I know that Cardinal Ricci said that my death would be hastened because I don't eat much,' she replied, 'but now the old fool himself is dead while I shall live for a century.'

Azzolini left Christina and went straight to the Englishman. He knew his man and simply placed a purse with a small amount of money in his hand.

'Now get out of Rome,' he ordered, 'for that is all you will ever get.'

The alchemist took the hint and was gone within two hours. Christina never made a single inquiry about him from that moment.

As usual, the Marquis del Monte emerged unscathed from the matter, and his business arrangement with the Englishman was revealed neither to Christina nor to Azzolini.

In fact, shortly after this Christina insisted on promoting del Monte to the resounding title of Great Master of the Horse and Major-Domo of the Household. This caused more fuss than she could understand.

Azzolini was the only person among the Cardinals and Ambassadors who would address the Marquis as Excellency, for he respected Christina's implicit belief that she had the undisputed right to appoint whom she liked in her own household.

Perhaps the Cardinal alone was large-minded enough to see that mere words affected the man's position but little, and that to bicker over a trivial honour in that pathetic little Court was to belittle oneself.

Azzolini was growing weary of so much gossip and commotion over del Monte.

He knew that in the final analysis he was the only person who really mattered to the Queen, and he realized also that despite this basic loyalty, she genuinely saw nothing wrong in rejecting his advice and dispensing with his companionship whenever she wished.

He was a patient man. He knew that in time the Marquis would fade from the scene, and again Dezio would be the only name on Christina's lips.

Yet as he listened to the reports of the adventurer's nefarious activities, he could not help but wonder how far away the end could be.

The Marquis had taken a small house opposite Christina's, but within the bounds of the privileged territory where diplomatic and police immunity existed.

He brought his long-suffering wife to live there, although he had not seen her for years.

This unusual regularity of his household did not curb his amorous activities, and he started a highly profitable organization which provided protection for women fleeing from justice.

Prostitutes who had fallen foul of the law, wives who had run away from their husbands, and daughters who had determined on a gayer life than a farm or tradesman's premises permitted, were welcomed.

All were expected to debauch themselves if they wanted to stay, and as it was a case of succumbing to the Marquis's advances or walking down the road and being arrested the decision was invariably the same.

Financial benefits came to the Marquis from the protection of robbers.

It cost them as much as twenty per cent of their booty to hire Christina's coach to take them beyond the borders of the Papal States. The same coach returned packed to the roof with goods on which duty was payable.

Both the outgoing criminals and the incoming contraband passed openly through the streets of Rome, the police and customs officers being powerless to stop the vehicle because it carried the Royal insignia.

Christina knew much of what was going on.

Indeed, the Marquis made a point of telling her the more amusing stories of his adventures, though omitting details of the pecuniary benefits which accrued. Her love of mischief influenced her to do nothing whatever about it.

Moreover, she had her usual implicit confidence that her own judgement was perfect and all the stories she heard to the Marquis's disadvantage were figments of his enemies' jealous imagination.

So complete was her trust in del Monte that she deputed him to inspect her properties in Sweden. This project was, not unexpectedly, a great success.

Current revenues for Christina had been passed through Hamburg regularly since the Diet's promise of reasonable behaviour, but the earlier monies were still outstanding.

The Marquis remained in Sweden for a year, cajoling, threatening and investigating.

He rapidly discovered the real situation, and promptly demanded that the numerous nobles and statesmen who had borrowed from the revenues should start repaying their loans.

He did, of course, take a percentage for himself on the money thus obtained, but Christina never examined the accounts, and she was only too happy to have anything at all.

After the Marquis had put Christina's affairs in a better order than they had been since her Abdication he made a protracted tour of the estates which yielded part of the Queen's pension.

He informed the tenants that he had been given powers by the Queen to turn out those who appeared to him to be poor farmers.

A few he did dismiss and gave their land to newcomers in return for an introductory fee. But most of the peasants and small farmers who had lived there for generations were told that he would grant a new lease for a consideration.

There were, of course, the inevitable scandals when he came across a pretty farmer's wife, and when he crossed over to Pomerania to investigate the accounts of Christina's estates there he narrowly escaped being murdered by a furious husband.

However, his tour was on the whole extremely successful, and he returned to his mistress the richer in experience, money, and glory.

In his cups he told some of his lady friends that he had made a personal profit of some thirty or forty thousand crowns from the Swedish tour.

This may have been an exaggeration, but he certainly had more money than he had ever known before in his long and disgraceful career.

His debaucheries amazed all Rome, not on account of their disgusting nature, but because they continued night after night for weeks. He was well into his sixties and the strain inevitably told on his physique.

One night at Christina's request he arranged a concert and afterwards started his own preferences in entertainment. In the early hours of the morning, after a hearty meal, he retired to sleep.

At eleven the next morning he arose and felt dizzy. He fell

down in a fit, and by the time Christina had been summoned to see him his face had swollen, the skin had turned nearly purple and foam covered his chin and chest.

The sight was so horrible that the Queen recoiled in fear and disgust.

'It looks as if the Devil is strangling him with invisible hands,' she whispered.

As she spoke the awful gurgling stopped and the eyes almost stood out of his head. The Marquis del Monte was dead.

Christina missed 'her naughty Marquis', as she called him more than she thought possible.

Azzolini was so deeply involved in the cares of State – virtually the whole political life of the Papal States depended on his attention – that he could only visit her in the evening, and then only as one of many names in his diary.

Christina needed companionship more than advice, a devotee more than a mentor.

The yearnings of her adolescence returned and were strengthened by a maternal feeling she did her best to disguise, for she still hated the very thought of pregnancy, and many a tearful woman had rushed from her presence because Christina had seen the signs of coming motherhood.

'You cow!' was the unworthy insult she hurled after them – and regretted it the moment the door was closed.

She used to salve her sense of guilt by sending them a lavish gift of money, but she would never countermand her order that any pregnant woman would be dismissed from her employment.

Now she sought out pretty little girls and attempted to train and educate them.

One was a beautiful country child named Giovannina who rapidly benefited from the lessons Christina gave her in good manners and correct speech.

Knowing the Queen's views on marriage Giovannina wisely kept her love affair with a young man in the French Embassy as secret as possible, until one day Christina tip-toed into her room and pounced on a letter she was writing.

Having read the letter Christina lost her temper and the girl in terror threw herself on the floor and begged forgiveness. White with anger the Queen walked away, and Giovannina sat miserably awaiting punishment.

Half an hour later Christina reappeared, smiling pleasantly, and handed the astonished girl her own idea of a love letter to copy.

She had poured out her heart in this letter even though she pretended that she was only playing a part in an amusing conspiracy to excite and mislead the young Frenchman.

For some time Christina became the brains behind the love affair; she devised the most passionate endearments and arranged trysts which, however, never permitted Giovannina and her lover to achieve any real intimacy.

A serenade to a balcony, a glimpse of one another from two facing windows, meetings at concerts – these were the only contacts Christina allowed.

Unfortunately, Giovannina was a highly sexed young woman, and while she had to obey the Queen as regards the young man at the French Embassy she met plenty of gallants who enjoyed the unconventional freedom of Christina's house.

She became pregnant through a liaison which flourished under the very nose of the Queen, and if Christina had not been so certain that the girl was slavishly devoted to her she must have known of it.

Christina's affection for Giovannina withstood the shock of the news of her fall from grace, but she insisted that the trouble should be remedied. Giovannina died as the result of the medicines which Christina gave her.

The Queen arranged for her to be buried with a chaplet of white flowers as a mark of virginity, and for days she wept in abject misery, shutting herself in her room and seeing nobody.

However, her mourning did not last, and as soon as she was about again, she looked for a new companion. The search did not take long.

Georgina Angelica was known in Rome as 'the Incomparable Virgin'.

It was stated on fairly reliable evidence that her father had been a high official of the Church, and certainly there was a remarkable nobility in the girl's exquisite countenance, which had little in common with the lowly state of her mother.

Georgina was tall and slender, with an oval face and sparkling eyes. She was reputedly the best singer in Rome and when Christina first saw her at a concert she caught her breath in wonder.

Her memory travelled back, stopped momentarily beside

the river in Lyons, and then rested in the candle-lit bedroom of the Stockholm Palace more than thirty years earlier.

The girl who was singing had the same pale bright flaxen hair which Christina had adored to stroke on Ebba Sparre's head.

As Christina did not want a similar experience to that which she had endured with Giovannina, she immediately made careful inquiries about Georgina.

She discovered that money had been lavishly provided for the girl's education, and that she had the advantages of good breeding as well as an unsurpassed knowledge of music.

Unfortunately, she was completely under the domination of her mother, who realized that her daughter's musical career would prove very lucrative, while eventually a successful marriage could be arranged.

Georgina was very unhappy for she had fallen in love with a young student, and there were constant quarrels at home when her mother reprimanded her for considering such a worthless union and urged her to pay attention to the numerous wealthy suitors who were constantly but vainly paying court to her.

At the time Christina was acquainting herself with the girl's life story, Georgina was so desolated that she had considered entering a convent.

The Queen instantly offered her the protection of her household, and the girl gratefully came as a maid-in-waiting the same day.

She was temperamentally very different from her predecessor. Christina quickly discovered that the love affair with the student was in reality a very mild friendship and that Georgina was literally panic-stricken at the very idea of a liaison with the worldly men her mother suggested.

The Queen believed that this lovely young life would comfort and invigorate her in her old age. The girl, on the other hand, was content to live in the serene and, to her, sexless companionship of a woman who was some years older than her mother.

Neither could possibly know that a ghostly, ominous figure stood invisible beside the lovely young girl who gave thanks in song for her good fortune before the entranced Christina.

The figure was Death.

CHAPTER FIFTEEN

CHRISTINA's devotion to Georgina, following on the rumours of her interference in Giovannina's amorous affairs, aroused far more scandal in sophisticated Rome than had been caused in the past by the infatuation between the Queen and Ebba. But it was not harsh criticism.

Many people were ready to regard Christina's interest as that of a rather motherly woman for an adopted daughter.

But others, in an endeavour to expound their wisdom on the trends of human psychology and the aberrations to which the mortal frame was subjected, claimed to have special knowledge of Christina's peculiarities.

These stories vastly amused Christina when they duly came to her ears. She bided her time for a chance to deny them.

One morning she was exercising a favourite horse by driving around the roads near her house in a light carriage.

A servant of the French Ambassador came to watch. Christina called out to him, demanding to know if she did not drive well.

The coachman loyally admitted that only the King of France could handle the reins so expertly.

Christina was annoyed at the reply. She whipped up the mare and turned into an exercising yard which adjoined her house. It was very small and the Queen turned so sharply that the carriage overturned, throwing her headlong and dis-arranging her clothes.

She was badly shaken and her ankle was twisted. Neither the French coachman nor her own stable-hands, who had come to watch the display, dared to approach her because her light summer dress had been almost torn off her, and she was lying semi-naked on the ground.

She saw their hesitancy and laughed at their embarrassment.

'Come and lift me up,' she called. 'I am not sorry that I am seen by this accident, to the end that it may be known that I am neither male nor hermaphrodite, as some people have passed me for.'

Needless to say, the story was all around Rome by that evening, and a rumour that had come and gone, but never died, ever since the cry of 'a son!' had been raised at her birth, was scotched for ever.

After that Christina dressed in a more womanly fashion than had hitherto been her custom, often selecting dresses which revealed much of her bosom.

This was at the time the height of fashion, for Clement IX permitted a tolerance in dress and encouraged pleasurable activities of the Arts which made his reign an all-too-brief Golden Age for Roman society.

He was Pontiff for only three years, dying from a stroke in December, 1670.

Even before his funeral Christina was excitedly discussing with Cardinal Azzolini the likely identity of his successor.

There were twenty-five men in the Catholic hierarchy who felt confident that they were the only possible candidates for the supreme position, but Christina knew of only one – Azzolini himself.

The tradition that it was the Divine Will that selected the candidate and named him through the members of the Conclave did not prevent an enormous amount of intrigue and argument. But at first the Queen would not even admit there were any other candidates in the running.

'When you are Pope you can look forward to twenty or thirty years of glory,' she told Azzolini.

He shook his head.

'That is precisely why there is no chance of my election. The Conclave fears the results of a long reign. At forty-seven I am at least twenty years too young to have a chance.'

He convinced Christina that their wisest course was to do everything possible to influence the election of a Pope favourable to them.

They agreed that the best would be their old friend, Cardinal Vidoni, to whom they owed a debt of gratitude for his efforts to put Christina on the throne of Poland.

The Cardinals in their little cells in the Vatican were supposedly held *incommunicado* so that the Divine Choice could be made through their voting slips without the corruption of worldly influence.

Christina, however, believed implicitly that God helps those who help themselves, and by means of the physician who attended to the Cardinals' medical needs, and the waiters who pushed trays of austere food through the grills of the cell doors she learned all she wanted to know.

Characteristically, she rejected unfavourable titbits of gossip and told Azzolini that everything was going well.

She was wrong. The Conclave elected the octogenarian Cardinal Alberi, who was so old and feeble that he hardly knew what was happening.

'He is said to lie in bed so long that his servants are never certain whether he is dead or alive,' complained Christina when Azzolini brought her the news. 'He won't live a month.'

She was wrong again. The old man surprised everybody by hanging on to life for six years.

He was content to let everything and everyone alone if he was left in peace, and for Christina the period was a delightful one. Rome gave itself up to masquerades, balls and concerts.

The Queen's star shone brightly in this artistic firmament, and there were none of these unfortunate reprimands from the Papal Authority when worldliness impinged too strongly on the activities and lives of her guests, a large number of whom were always exalted members of the Church.

On the death of Clement X in 1676 the situation altered rapidly.

The new Pope, who took the title of Innocent XI, had been a vague acquaintance of Christina and Azzolini in earlier years when he was Cardinal Odescalchi. Real friendliness had been impossible because of his asceticism and dislike of luxury.

On his accession Rome soon discovered that the easy-going times under the previous two Popes was at an end.

Gambling dens, women singers, and revealing dress were among the first things forbidden by Innocent XI. It was said that he spent most of his day lying on a hard cot in contemplation, and he wept so constantly at the wickedness of the world around him that many people genuinely believed that he suffered from some disease of the eyes.

He was obviously not a man with whom Christina had much in common. Besides, he was the darling of France, and this was sufficient to antagonize her.

What was more she made no secret of her contempt of his reforms.

The Pope returned the compliment by cancelling the pension the Vatican had promised her for life. True, it was not entirely an individually spiteful action.

He cut out a large number of similar private incomes paid to Papal relatives, their families and their descendants.

Yet Christina had perforce to admire his uncompromising uprightness and courage when a serious dispute arose with Louis XIV, who had not unreasonably expected that a man he had always favoured in every way would be amenable.

Louis was head of the Church in France by privilege of birth, and he claimed the right to take the revenues and appoint his favourite priests to benefices in vacant bishoprics.

The Pope disputed this right and threatened to excommunicate any priest appointed by the King of France in the diocese of Palmiers, in Languedoc.

Louis accepted the challenge, and called an assembly of the French clergy who passed four Articles, the most notable of which was that Papal Decrees were null and void in France if the French Church, or rather its Head, the King, did not approve of them.

The crisis naturally stimulated Christina as trouble always did. She became almost friendly with the Pope and urged him to assert his authority.

Innocent XI really needed no urging, and the dispute between the Vatican and Versailles dragged on until long after both rulers were dead.

Christina's truce with the Holy Father was short-lived.

The Pope started a campaign to curb the drunkenness of the city, and the police had special orders to arrest all the vendors of smuggled spirits who were the principal source of the lavish supplies of alcohol obtained by the common people.

When a brandy smuggler was being pursued by the police on Easter morning he turned into the grounds of Christina's palace for sanctuary.

The police ignored the Queen's diplomatic privilege, and rushed through the gates, cornering their quarry in the stable-yard. Christina, returning from Mass, saw a crowd at the side of the house, and went to investigate.

The vendor was hanging on to the bolts on a stable door while two policemen were trying to force him to yield by strangling him with a rope.

Christina ordered two of her own bodyguard to rescue the man and kick the police off her premises.

The Pope was given a report of the affair. He ordered the Treasurer to inaugurate legal proceedings against the men who had assaulted the police. The official thereupon issued a decree condemning the men to death in their absence.

This was the sort of insolent challenge Christina enjoyed. She wrote a personal letter to the Treasurer and which was designed to annoy the Pope as much as him.

'Dishonouring yourself and your master by what you call justice,' she wrote, 'I am sorry for you now and shall be still more so when you are a Cardinal. In the meantime I give you my words that those whom you have condemned to death shall, please God, yet live a little longer; and should they chance to die by other than a natural death they shall not die alone.'

The next morning there was great bustle in the courtyard of the Queen's household.

The strongly guarded gates opened and the whole of Christina's suite emerged with the Queen walking at the head. Men armed to the teeth protected the two condemned guards and the brandy vendor.

Christina chose the Jesuits' church for her devotions that day, partly because it necessitated a walk through several main streets and also because she knew that the Order disliked the Pope.

The discomfited Vatican police watched her helplessly, not daring to start a brawl which would inevitably involve the Queen, who was herself brandishing a pistol.

Day after day she repeated this armed foray until the Pope withdrew all police from the route.

She was rather sorry that she had won so easily.

'I am like Caesar of old,' she told a worried Azzolini. 'I walk among pirates, and like him, I menace them, and they fear me.'

The Cardinal ever-mindful of the financial factors of her life, reminded her that her attitude left him little chance of getting the pension from the Vatican restored – a matter on which he had been working patiently.

'I assure you,' she told him, 'that the end of that pension was the most pleasant news in the world to me. The 12,000 crowns allowed me by the Pope were the sole blot on my life, and I took them as a mortification from the hand of God in order to lower my pride; I see well He has taken me into His Grace by His singular favour of removing them.'

All the Cardinal could do was to smile. Christina was beginning to look old, but the youthful ebullience which had fascinated him when they first met still invigorated her spirit.

She would always be young in heart and because of it he knew he would always be her slave.

It could have once been said that the world was divided into two parties: those who followed Rome and exulted in Christina's conversion and those who staunchly supported the Protestant faith and detested her.

In the evening of her life the old religious wounds were healed by the lapse of time. The disgust at her behaviour and those around her lessened as it was accepted that she meant no harm.

Christina did not really change. She was, with reason, convinced of her intellectual superiority over her contemporaries. By right of birth she had learned to treat the world with the coldness of her exalted rank.

This sentiment was strengthened by the deep hurt she felt when the whole world, enemies and friends alike, misunderstood her motives in abdication.

She never forgot nor forgave the general belief that because of a temperamental nature and an hysterical desire for notoriety she had thrown away her heritage on a whim of eccentricity.

'I was born with an insatiable curiosity for knowledge,' she said to Azzolini one evening as they commemorated the date of her abdication. 'I always felt impelled to test the truth of everything for myself, and truly it has been rare when I have not wanted to reject what I heard and saw.'

'You are a Vasa,' the Cardinal answered gently. 'The disharmony of your mind shows that the blood of your ancestors controls you more strongly than the spirit of your newly adopted faith.'

It was rare for the Queen to make an explosive retort when Azzolini was frank with her, as was her custom when others annoyed her with far less direct charges.

All she did was to laugh a little and protest that to call a conversion of more than twenty years' duration a newly adopted faith was unjust.

Yet he was perfectly correct.

Perhaps Christina's sudden and ill-timed bouts of hysterical misbehaviour came from her neurotic mother, but her proud and incorruptible individualism was in the exact tradition of her father and his ancestors.

'What must the ghosts of the Vasa kings be saying of me now?' was one of Christina's favourite comments when she took part in some historic Catholic ceremony.

Her listeners wondered at her temerity, but she knew instinctively that the incorruptible and forceful ancestors who had formed her character were probably rejoicing in the career of the last of their direct line.

Despite all the trouble she had brought to her country, she had acted just as a Vasa should.

She pursued her convictions regardless of others' opinions; she kept a cynical mind which cut like a razor through falsity when she was really intent on making a true analysis.

She was absolutely certain that the voices within her head which drove her remorselessly to search for truth were better mentors than the wisest and kindest of the men around her.

In the closing years of her life, Christina was probably more liked in Rome than ever before. It was said that of all the antiquities in the city she was the most intriguing.

She had become very plump, and with her double chin and bright little eyes, and her fair hair only slightly flecked with grey, her face was more attractive than it had ever been in her youth.

She maintained her spirit to the end and took every opportunity she could find to cause discussion by her controversial remarks. Typical of them was her comment on the Papacy.

'The Church must certainly be governed by the Holy Ghost,' she exclaimed, 'for since I have been in Rome, I have seen four Popes and I swear that not one of them had any common sense whatever.'

In February, 1689 she was stricken with malaria and during the illness erysipelas broke out. For some days she hovered between life and death, but to everybody's surprise she slowly recovered.

The experience softened her attitude and when she was up and about again, walking rather slowly in her garden during the first warm days of spring, she told her confessor that she believed she had some years yet to live.

'God has snatched me from the arms of death against my own expectation,' she told him. 'I thought I was on my inevitable last journey, but here I am full of life. The strength of my constitution had surmounted an illness capable of killing twenty Hercules. I hope to be quite well by Easter.'

In April she fell ill again. Georgina was her nurse and rarely left her bedside day or night.

But one evening, when Christina was dozing, she left the bedroom to go to her own which adjoined the Queen's. To the girl's amazement a table had been laid there for supper, and her mother was sitting in a chair by the window.

'Come, child, you must eat,' she said.

Georgina was a little mystified at this unexpected visit as her mother took very little interest in her since she had joined the Queen's household. She was still more bewildered at the unwonted regard for her well-being.

She sat down and began to eat, for she was hungry after a long day of nursing the Queen. Her mother went to the door and opened it.

She beckoned to a renegade abbot named Vannini who had been importuning the girl for months. The priest entered and the older woman slipped out, leaving the two alone.

Georgina cried out in alarm and ran to the corner of the room. The abbot lurched after her. The table went over with a crash. Servants rushed in, and Vannini escaped after a struggle.

Christina staggered out of bed on hearing the noise but fell to the floor.

She demanded to know what was happening, and her servants made any excuse they could. She then called for Georgina.

Azzolini had in the meantime arrived and he begged the girl not to divulge the facts because of the inevitable effect on the Queen's health. Georgina was however suffering from shock so she did not listen to him.

Crying hysterically, she threw herself on Christina's bed and begged for protection from her unnatural mother and her would-be seducer.

The Queen demanded the truth from Azzolini. He mumbled something and she knew he was lying.

By threatening that she would get out of bed and visit the servants' quarters she forced him to agree that she should interview them privately one by one. And from their evidence she pieced together the real facts.

Next morning, outwardly calm and seemingly a little better,

Christina summoned her most trusted officer of the guard and placed a purse of gold in his hand.

'Go out and find this man Vannini,' she ordered. 'Bring me his head, and don't return until you have it.'

The officer discovered that the terrified abbot had fled from Rome, constantly changing carriages to cover his flight.

He traced him as far as Naples where influential friends of Vannini bribed him with a thousand crowns to hold his hand.

The officer, worrying about his own fate if the Queen should soon die and leave him undefended on a charge of murder, agreed to pretend that his quarry had escaped. He returned to Rome.

Christina was much weaker. But his story put her in such a rage that she leaped out of bed, scratching his face and raining blows on his body. She got her hands round his throat and was strangling him when she fell unconscious.

That evening, with Georgina kneeling at the bedside and Azzolini standing beside her sponging her forehead with vinegar, Christina quite calmly said that she knew she was dying as the result of the exertion to avenge her 'dear companion'.

She asked that a messenger be sent to the Pope, to ask his forgiveness for the harsh expressions which she had allowed to escape because of her hasty temper.

The Pope sent her Absolution on her last evening of life but did not visit her in person.

She died shortly after dawn on 19 April, 1689.

She had made her will a few weeks earlier, and apart from small bequests to a few friends, the Pope, the Kings of France and Spain and the Elector of Brandenburg, she left everything she had to her beloved Azzolini.

This she said was because of his incomparable qualities, his personal merit and his services for so many years. She stipulated that with her bequest he should provide 20,000 Masses to be said for her soul.

She had not forgotten Georgina.

Secretly, because of the legal problems involved in taking a girl out of the control of her vicious mother, Christina had arranged for the Duchess of Medina Celi, wife of the Spanish Ambassador, to take her into her personal employment.

The kindly woman came tiptoeing to the bedside during the night as Christina lay sinking into death. Georgina's skirts rustled when she stood up and the Queen opened her eyes. She smiled at her ward and made a slight gesture of her hand towards her.

It was the last conscious movement she made.

Azzolini was heartbroken at the Queen's death, and he only survived her for two months. There was, in fact, very little money after her debts had been paid and most of her furniture and personal effects were bought by the noble families of Rome.

They then managed to evade paying for them because of the upheaval when the Cardinal died and, although his nephew claimed to be the legatee, there was much uncertainty as to who was actually the legal owner.

The Pope bought the library and collection of manuscripts for the Vatican.

Christina had left instructions that there should be no ostentatious celebrations at her funeral and that her tomb should be a simple one.

However, the Pope saw fit to ignore these wishes and the funeral rites included an enormous procession to St. Peter's, where her embalmed body was buried in the Basilica.

He also gave instructions for a large memorial to be erected within the church, but this was not completed until after he had died the same autumn.

The three deaths brought down the curtain and ended the tragi-comedy so abruptly that by New Year, 1690, Christina was already just a memory in Rome.

The amazement at her caprices, her vanity, and her prodigality evaporated. None of the activities into which she had poured her heart and soul had any real effect on the political scene of seventeenth-century Europe.

Curiously enough, however, one of the rare opportunities which she failed to grasp sent its echoes down the passage of time to mould the history of the twentieth century – an era of great wars, of social upheaval, and of noted individuals revolting against the accepted social code, so similar to the age in which she herself had lived.

'The Polish Diet have preferred a weak Prince,' Christina said to Azzolini when the news of her failure to gain the Polish Crown was known. 'They are fools, for they do not see that a strong neighbour will thereby feel it safe to make himself stronger.

'We Swedes know the Prussians. Mark my words, when the Hohenzollerns no longer respect the discipline of their Polish suzerain, all Europe will have cause to tremble.'

The Cardinal, lacking the ability to see the broad horizon of Northern politics, cared little about the Elector of Brandenburg busily fashioning the history of Prussia.

He dismissed Christina's opinion as yet another example of her sense of the dramatic, and her innate inability to consider politics dispassionately.

Yet Christina on the throne of Sweden would certainly have avoided the disastrous wars that weakened Sweden's sway over her Prussian vassal.

And she would have had a second chance to curb the vaunting ambition of that aggressive nation if she had guided a resolute Poland.

Her actions were invariably of little consequence but in her inaction she fashioned the future for us in the twentieth century.

BIBLIOGRAPHY

Axel Oxenstierna. W. Tham. 1935.

Background to Sweden. Terence Heywood.

Christina of Sweden. Margaret Goldsmith.

Christina of Sweden. Ada Harrison. 1929.

Christina, Queen of Sweden. F. W. Bain. 1890.

Christine von Schweden. Hannah Szaz. 1930.

Court of Christina of Sweden, The. Francis Gribble. 1913.

Deux Enigmas Historiques. Ernest Rénan. 1923.

Drottming Christina. Curt Weibull. 1931.

Faltmarkskalarna Johan Baner och Lennart Torstensson. L. Tingstein. 1932.

Gustav Adolf. Johannes Paul. 1932.

Gustavus Adolphus and the Struggle of Protestantism for Existence. C. R. L. Fletcher. 1892.

Histoire de la Vie de la Reyne Christine de Suède. Anon. 1677.

History of the Intrigues and Gallantries of Christina. Anon. 1697.

History of the Popes. Ranke.

History of the Swedes. E. G. Geiger. 1845.

Istoria di Christina. Count Galeazzo Gualdo. 1656.

Journal of the Swedish Embassy. Bulstrode Whitelocke. 1654.

King Gustav of Sweden. Basil Herbert. 1938.

Lettres inédités de Christine et le Cardinal Azzolini. Baron de Bildt. 1899.

Lovely Land, The. S. F. A. Coles. 1949.

Memoires de Chanut. 1675.

Mémoires of Christina. Henry Woodhead. 1863.

Memoires de Christine, Reine de Suède. Arckenholtz. 1770.

Memoirs of Christina. Henry Woodhead. 1863.

Première Visite de Christine de Suède a la Cour de France. F. Wrangel. 1908.

Saint Birgitta. Edith Peacey. 1933.

Scandinavia. Eric de Maré. 1952.

Scandinavians in History, The. S. M. Toyne.

Short History of Sweden. A Ragnar Svanstro and Carl
   Fredrik Palmstierna.
Sibyl of the North, The. Faith Compton Mackenzie. 1931.
Siècle de Louis XIV. Voltaire.
Sveriges Historia. E. Hildebrand. 1926.
Swedish Intelligencer, The. 1633.
Swedish Miniatures. August Strindberg.
Thirty Years War, The. S. R. Gardiner. 1892.
Thirty Years War, The. C. V. Wedgwood. 1938.
Wallenstein und der Osten. R. Lorenz. 1934.

BANNERS OF LOVE BY SACHA CARNEGIE

part 1 of the trilogy DESTINY OF EAGLES

Kasia was proud, high spirited, beautiful . . . the only daughter of the Radienski family, landowners to the vast Ukrainian estate of Volochisk. Destined to love only one man – Henryk – her life was brutally shattered when Turkish marauders swept over the land, butchering her family and carrying her south to serve as concubine in the seraglio of Diran Bey. And when at last she made her escape, it was to find herself once more the victim of a man's desire – Pugachev – barbaric leader of the Cossack horde, who demanded she should be his 'wife' . . .

Through violence, passion and intrigue, Kasia came at last to the glitter of the Grand Ducal Court in St. Petersburg . . . here again to meet the man she loved . . .

0 552 09520 6   40p

THE BANNERS OF POWER BY SACHA CARNEGIE

part 3 of the trilogy DESTINY OF EAGLES

It had been five long years since beautiful Kasia Radienski had seen or heard of the man she loved – her childhood sweetheart, Henryk Barinski. Five years of bloodshed and revolution in which she had served as friend and lady-in-waiting to Catherine, Empress of Russia. And then, one day, a letter arrived from Henryk, revealing that he had escaped from Siberia, where, in the continual darkness of the torture cells, he had suffered greatly at the hands of the Russians.

And now that he was back in their native Poland, Kasia was determined that nothing should prevent her from going to him – not even the Empress of Russia . . .

0 552 09522 2   40p

THE BANNERS OF WAR BY SACHA CARNEGIE

part 2 of the trilogy DESTINY OF EAGLES

One bitter Siberian night in the winter of 1758, Henryk Barinski escaped from the imprisonment to which the Russian Secret Chancellery had sentenced him. Helped by fur-trappers, he made his way to England, but before he could reach London he was press-ganged into service on a British ship. The Seven Years' War was raging, and Henryk experienced the sweltering carnage of battle as well as the disease and brutalities which were then all part of a sailor's life in the Royal Navy.

Despite all the horrors he witnessed, his childhood companion and lover, Kasia, was never far from his thoughts. At the end of the war, Henryk received news which made him determined to rejoin her and return to his beloved Poland ...

0 552 09521 4   40p

CHARLES I BY CHRISTOPHER HIBBERT

Christopher Hibbert provides a highly readable account of the life, times and elusive personality of a man still regarded by some as a martyr. He faithfully reproduces the world of Charles I, his court, his artistic patronage and his family life, while tracing the course of events that led to his execution.

'He is urbane, shrewd and economical; in a tightly organized book he makes every sentence count.' – *Observer*

0 552 09066 2   75p

A SELECTED LIST OF CORGI AUTOBIOGRAPHIES AND BIOGRAPHIES FOR YOUR READING PLEASURE

All these books are available at your bookshop or newsagent: or can be ordered direct from the publisher. Just tick the titles you want and fill in the form below.

CORGI BOOKS, Cash Sales Department, P.O. Box 11, Falmouth, Cornwall.

Please send cheque or postal order. No currency, and allow 10p to cover the cost of postage and packing (plus 5p each for additional copies).

NAME (Block letters) ....

ADDRESS ....

(SEPT 74) ....

While every effort is made to keep prices low, it is sometimes necessary to increase prices at short notice. Corgi Books reserve the right to show new retail prices on covers which may differ from those previously advertised in the text or elsewhere.